Names Will ~~Never~~ Hurt Me: Healing for Victims of Bullying

Mark A. Stewart

Dauntless Press

Winston-Salem, North Carolina

Published in 2016 by Dauntless Press, Winston-Salem, North Carolina, USA

ISBN-10: 0-9972819-0-1
ISBN-13: 978-0-9972819-0-3

Library of Congress Cataloging-in-publication data:
Stewart, Mark A
Names Will Hurt Me: Healing for Victims of Bullying / by: Mark A. Stewart - 1st edition

Edited by: Kit Duncan
Cover Design by: Maria Gandolfo

Dauntless Press
Winston-Salem, NC

Acknowledgments

There have been so many people who helped make this project a reality.

Mike McClanahan and Kit Duncan were tough editors who pushed me to not settle, and make the book all it could be. Maria Gandolfo did an amazing job designing a cover that is not only visually appealing, but stays true to the core message of the book.

A special thank you to Susan Westbrook for her coaching and encouragement when I was close to giving up on finishing the book.

Rudy Anderson has been a good friend, mentor and is helping me promote the book to help others.

Thank you to my friends and family who supported me, and put up with hearing endless updates and chatter about this project.

Most of all, I want to thank my amazing wife, Tina. She has been my biggest supporter and my inspiration. Her love gave me the strength and perseverance to see this through till it was published. She is the love of my life.

Disclaimer

For Educational and Informational Purposes Only. The information provided in this book is not intended to be a substitute for professional medical advice, diagnosis or treatment that can be provided by your own Medical Provider, Mental Health Provider, or member of the clergy. Therefore, do not disregard or delay seeking professional medical, mental health or religious advice because of information you have read in this book. Do not stop taking any medications without speaking to your own Medical Provider or Mental Health Provider. If you have or suspect that you have a medical or mental health problem, contact your own Medical Provider or Mental Health Provider promptly.

Contents

Introduction..........7

Section 1 - My Story and Long-term Effects

1.   My Story..........13
2.   Long-term Effects..........31

Section 2 - Negative Coping Mechanisms

3.   The Underachiever..........37
4.   The Overachiever..........47
5.   The People Pleaser..........55
6.   The Punisher..........65
7.   More Coping Mechanisms..........71

Section 3 - Roadmap to the Life You Desire

8.   The Ultimate Road Trip..........81
9.   Unpacking the Car..........85
10.   Deep Cleaning..........89
11.   The Out of Balance Victim Mentality..........101
12.   Balancing the Tires..........107
13.   Reprogramming Your GPS..........115
14.   Deciding on a Destination..........129
15.   Roadblocks..........147
16.   Rest Stops..........157
17.   Fun and Physical Exercise..........165
18.   Gratitude and Service..........173
19.   Religious Affiliation..........181
20.   Meditation/Prayer..........185
21.   Personal Inventory and Flow..........189
        Conclusion..........193

        Resources..........197
        Bibliography..........198
        About the Author..........203

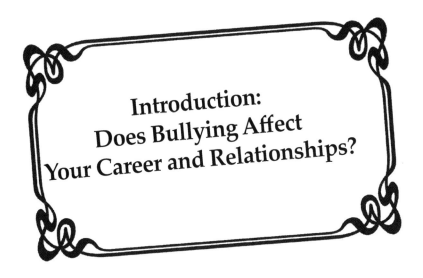

Introduction:
Does Bullying Affect
Your Career and Relationships?

Over the last couple of decades media coverage has focused a lot of attention on bullying in schools. It's great that bullying in schools is finally being taken seriously, but what if you were bullied in school and are still having issues as an adult? Until recently bullying was marginalized, along with your pain. You were told things like, "kids will be kids," "it's just part of growing up" and "bullying is not that bad." When you were in the midst of the bullying, some adults even told you that you needed to toughen up or fight back.

These adults didn't understand that the bullies were often physically much stronger and faster, or that they had enough social clout to influence or coerce other kids to join them. Fighting back is foolish when you are outmatched and outnumbered.

The few adults who tried to help often unwittingly made things worse. The bullies waited until the adults weren't around and retaliated against you for being a snitch. The message was clear that any attempt to get an adult involved would result in much greater levels of abuse. The realization that you couldn't rely on anyone else made you feel more isolated and hopeless.

After graduating and getting away from the bullies, you wanted to move on with your life. But the years of abuse had taken their toll. Deep inside you may have still felt inadequate. You wanted the anger and pain to go away, but these feelings followed you into adulthood.

I understand these issues because I lived them. I was bullied for nine years, which left me with intense anger, periodic bouts of depression and a negative self-image. As you will see, my self-loathing and anger towards others destroyed every positive relationship in my life. It was more than ten years after I left high school before I began to heal from the abuse.

My struggle to overcome the psychological damage from the bullying led me to write this book. I want to help you and others heal from the pain inflicted by the bullies. My goals for this book are to:

- Validate your pain
- Illustrate how the psychological damage from the trauma can sabotage your career and relationships if not dealt with
- Help you begin the healing process and provide you with a road map to build the life you desire

Despite what you might have been told, bullying is more than part of growing up. Bullying is abuse by your peers. You experienced traumatic abuse at the very point of your life that you were beginning to separate from your parents. Your self-image was determined more by your peers than your parents. The bullies not only physically and/or verbally abused you, they stole from you. Every incident of bullying was one positive memory from your childhood that you were denied. If the bullying was pervasive enough, you might feel like you were robbed of nearly every positive memory from your school years. When you look back at the years in middle

school or high school, you might only see pain and torment.

The first section in this book shows the long-term effects that bullying can have on you and other victims. Research and my story will be used to illustrate how much damage bullying does to your psyche and why you may still struggle with issues as an adult.

The second section of the book reveals several negative coping mechanisms and personas that you and other victims often utilize that can inhibit healing and keep you trapped in a downward spiral in your career and relationships. You will likely see yourself in more than one of these coping mechanisms to varying degrees. When you finish this section you will have a better understanding of the effects the abuse might have had on you psychologically and the ways these negative effects manifest themselves in your personality, thoughts, words and actions.

The last section of the book provides a roadmap to guide you through the healing process and begin the road trip towards the life you desire. There is information about roadblocks that can impede your progress, ways to maintain your vehicle to avoid problems and rest stops where you can relax and get back on course.

Not everyone will need to start the road trip from the same place. You may find that you have already moved past certain aspects of the bullying and only need to focus on parts of the healing process. You might also discover that the damage done was substantial enough that you need professional help to overcome your issues. You might need to see a professional counselor for issues you can't seem to get past. A counselor who utilizes Cognitive Behavioral Therapy (CBT) may be particularly useful.

Bullies often travel in small groups. If the bullies are leaders of social groups they pressure other students to join them out of fear of becoming targets themselves. These students

are sometimes referred to as bully-victims because they are put in the position of bullying others and may be victimized themselves. These students give the leader of the group(s) more power. Bully-victims struggle with the trauma from the bullying they experienced and the abuse they were forced to inflict on other victims. Both victims and bully-victims are much more likely to struggle with depression and anxiety disorders as adults, as well as being at higher risk of suicide (Pappas, 2013).

You are not the only one still struggling with issues from bulling you experienced in middle school or high school. Statistics show that "one out of every 4 kids will be bullied sometime throughout their adolescence" (Student Reports of Bullying, 2013). Some people are able to leave the trauma behind, but many still struggle as adults.

If this book is helpful in your recovery, please send me a note and let me know. You will find resources in the back of the book including online resources and links to organizations. Several of these organizations provide information on local support groups and therapists to aid you in your attempts to get beyond the damage from the bullying.

Section 1
My Story and
Long-term Effects

Chapter 1
My Story

As a former victim of bullying, I am too familiar with how painful it is to be under the complete control of another person who wants to inflict physical and/or mental pain on you. If you were a victim of bullying, you understand the shame of being humiliated in front of others and the strange way that you may have internalized the shame and anger. You likely have struggled as an adult with issues related to the bullying. One study showed that, "Beyond the immediate trauma of experiencing bullying, victims are at high risk of later physical and emotional disorders" (Vanderbilt and Augustyn, 2010).

It is the feeling of being completely under the control of someone else, a person who is intent on inflicting pain and suffering, that leaves such deep scars. The bullies relied on larger physical stature, social power within a group or sheer intimidation to make you feel powerless to fight back. This gave the bullies total control. It wasn't just one incident, over time they broke you down. That eventually allowed the bullies to inflict physical and/or verbal abuse without any resistance. It not only made you feel helpless, it took away your hope. You were left with a sense that you had no control over your own life and were unable to change your circumstances. If you have no power to bring about change in your life, why try?

I understand how you can still feel like a victim years or even decades after the abuse stopped. The years of being told you are less valuable than everyone else took their toll. Deep inside you may still feel inadequate. You want the pain and anger to go away, but these feelings have become such a part of your psyche that you don't know how to let go of them. People will often tell you to just get over it. You want to get beyond the pain from the past, but it isn't that simple. The bullies did serious damage to your self-esteem and made you feel less valuable than your peers.

Nine years of bullying left me with a negative self-image, a dull ache that was always with me and a rage bubbling under the surface. I longed to be free from the pain that was eating away at me deep inside. As the rage destroyed every good thing in my life, I came to the realization that I needed some form of emotional healing. I fantasized that I would magically be "healed" and all my problems would be solved. The past and the trauma I endured at the hands of the bullies would never haunt me again. I pictured myself like Julie Andrews, standing at the top of a hill with my arms stretched high as "The Sound of Music" burst forth around me. This "healing" would be a magical place, and I would finally be free.

I discovered that reality almost never resembles fantasy as I searched for healing. Emotional pain doesn't always heal on its own. As the victim spends years replaying the abuse, the pain may intensify rather than heal. Sometimes the pain is so intense that the victim feels that the only way out is to end his/her life. For example, on September 9, 2013, twelve year old Rebecca Ann Sedwick jumped off of a concrete silo after being bullied for over nine months by two girls. In May 2013, Katlin Loux hanged herself after more than two years of being bullied in school (Wilson, 2013), and in September 2010, Tyler Clementi jumped off a bridge after his college roommate recorded him in a gay sexual encounter without his knowledge and posted it online (Weiner-Bronner, 2010). These are only a few out of hundreds or thousands of suicides that happen every year as a result of bullying. The CDC (Center for Disease Control) says that "Suicide is the third leading cause of death among young people, resulting in about 4,400 deaths per year" and one study in Brittan found that "at least half of suicides among young people are related to bullying" (Bullying Statistics, 2015).

The bullying begins

I could have been a story in the local paper as well. As a young child, my family moved to a tiny town in the southern part of Illinois. The town had only 350 people who seemed to be related to each other. Close-knit communities like this can be tougher to fit into than impersonal cities, especially for an eight year old who stood three inches shorter and weighed ten pounds less than most of my peers. I was skinny, physically awkward and a poor athlete. These traits made me an easy target. For years I was "wimp," "fag" and "weakling."

High school came with a whole new level of bullying and abuse. Kids from the entire county went to one central high school. There were only approximately 100 students in my freshman class, but I was the second smallest male out of the group. Some of the bullies, who had been popular from my middle school, quickly established themselves near the top of the social heap. Within the first couple of weeks of high school this group more than doubled in size as the bullies from the smaller middle schools formed alliances. I was one

of the students this larger group singled out for abuse.

The verbal bullying ramped up quickly. Instead of "Stewart" I was called "Sewer" or "Sewage." At the beginning of the school year, I was making great grades but this seemed to incense the bullies. They added "stupid" and "retard" to the list of names in an apparent attempt to bring me down.

The physical abuse also increased in high school. The bullies had conditioned me to duck when one of them raised their hand quickly. If my reaction was adequate, the bully would run his fingers through his hair as if he were combing it and walk away laughing. That was more humiliating than when they actually hit me. I felt like such a coward for ducking for no reason at all. It made me feel less than human, like a beaten dog that cowers when its owner picks up a stick. I told myself how much of a coward I was as I walked away. Shame, guilt and anger washed over me as I tried to maintain some outward measure of dignity.

Occasionally, I couldn't take it anymore and I refused to duck. This would result in being hit in the forehead. The bullies always traveled in small groups. If I tried to stand up to one of them another would smack me on the head from behind. They surrounded me and slapped me till they appeared to get bored. As I dropped my books and covered my head, one of bullies would kick my stuff across the hallway. They would be laughing and joking as they walked away. No matter what reaction I gave, I ended up feeling like a coward and heaped more abuse on myself in addition to the torment from the bullies.

One person in particular would walk behind me on the stairs and push hard. There were times I tumbled down several steps and multiple kids kicked me as they walked by; not hard enough to do permanent damage, but enough to make me curl up in the fetal position. I would close my eyes and curl my body up into as small of a ball as I could. I wasn't just warding off the physical blows; I was trying desperately to disappear and not feel the shame that washed over me. If I close my eyes, I can still feel the kicks hitting my back and legs, see their smiles and hear the laughter echoing in my ears.

I hid the bruises from my parents and school officials but there were a few times my parents noticed. Since I was clumsy, it was easy to say that I fell or bumped into something. The mental anguish and anger were much more difficult to hide. My parents and the few friends I had made in a neighboring town where my mom went to church seemed to notice. They often asked me what was wrong, but my reply was always, "Nothing."

I tried getting help from teachers early in my freshman year. A handful of the bullies were pulled into the principal's office, but it was my word against theirs. They laughed as they walked out of the principal's office with no repercussions at all. As lunch began, two of the bullies pushed me into a corner and one of them hit me in the stomach several times. They shoved me in a locker and didn't let me out till lunch ended. I am mildly claustrophobic and being that long in such a small place left me in a panic attack. I was soaked with sweat when I went to the next class. My panic and having to go to class looking like I had run a marathon during lunch seemed to amuse many of my classmates. I learned that turning them in would be dealt with harshly.

Much of the bullying blurs together, but certain incidents were humiliating enough that the memories are still painful to think about. A part of me refused to give in to the abuse, and occasionally I would attempt to fight back. In the spring of my freshman year, I got an opportunity. The bullies had continued to mature physically much more rapidly than I had. They ran over me in basketball, football and most other sports. In PE class, when the teams were formed the captains would argue over who had to accept me on their team. They

made it crystal clear in front of everyone that my presence on a team meant a much higher chance of losing. It was humiliating.

I did, however, find that I could be successful on the tennis court. I found that I didn't have to be physically big to play well. I had one friend in town and he was a tennis player. We played every chance we got and I learned to play pretty well. My heart swelled in P.E. class when I was the first one picked for a change. I also hit a couple of the bullies pretty hard with tennis balls. None of them said anything on the court with the P.E. teacher close by, but the way they looked at me seemed to promise retribution.

We had to run around part of the school on the way into the building. Several of the bullies ran past me and took turns knocking me onto the ground or into bushes when the P.E teacher couldn't see them. By the time I made it to the locker room, I had several bruises and a lot of scratches.

Once inside the locker room, the bullies upped the game. Being snapped with wet towels in the shower was a daily event. But this time several of them circled around me, and took turns snapping me with wet towels. I managed to get into a corner of the large shower room and tried to cover myself as much as possible.

Standing there naked in the shower, cowering in the corner struggling to protect myself, was humiliating. I was covered with red welts when I finally ran out of the shower. I got dressed as quickly as I could and ran up the stairs towards the gym. I was afraid that if I didn't make it out of the locker room in time, they would find another way to torture me. As I got to the top of the stairs, I paused to gather myself and stop the tears that were welling up from deep inside. Feelings of fear, humiliation and physical pain washed over me, leaving me nauseous and almost dizzy. I felt like a coward for running away, but I was outnumbered. The pain from the welts, bruises and scratches finally hit me, and I winced as I walked into the gym.   I thought about going to a teacher, but I knew better than to report what happened.

That incident was the last straw. I stopped caring about school or much of anything else and my grades plummeted. The guidance counselor seemed to know I was capable of more. For the rest of my high school tenure, I was told many times that I should be making straight A's and how disappointed the teachers were with my performance. They still put me in the advanced classes, which had the same small group of students. My family was poor and most of these kids had money. They knew I couldn't afford a car or to go out on the weekends so they bragged loudly to each other about their cars and the fun they had on the weekends. They made sure I knew that I heard them and they used these taunts as another way to inflict abuse.

As cruel as the abuse from the boys was, it was the abuse by the girls that hurt the worst. There was one very pretty girl who I wanted to date, but I knew she wouldn't go out with me. As I was walking by her locker, one of the other girls asked, "Why don't you go out with Sewer?" She loudly said, "Eww," and they broke out in laughter. As they walked away they talked loudly about how gross it would be to go out with me. What little dignity and self-worth I was clinging to seemed to be sucked out of me like salt pulling the moisture out of a slug. This scenario or a similar one was repeated over and over again. By the end of my freshman year, I truly believed that no woman would ever be interested in me. I started to believe that my biggest fear, being alone, would be my future.

I tried harder to blend into the background. The less attention I drew to myself and the less others noticed me the better. In fact, I truly wanted to become invisible. I hid in corners or beside the rows of lockers between classes to keep

from being noticed. Even simple eye contact would get unwanted attention. I looked down at the floor and walked as fast as I could. It lessened the frequency of the torment but it didn't stop the bullies from occasionally hitting me, kicking me, spitting on me or telling me that I was worthless and would never amount to anything. Despite the old saying, "Sticks and stones may break my bones, but words will never hurt me," it's the words that do the most damage. After years of being told that I was worthless, I started believing it.

I am naturally a very outgoing person. Having to remain silent was like a prison. Every day I felt nauseous as I got on the bus. The nausea increased as the bus neared the high school and I would fight to not throw up as I got off the bus. My day began with getting to my locker quickly and finding a corner where nobody could see me to nervously wait for the class bell to ring. The remainder of the day was spent walking fast with my head down and ducking when one of the bullies raised their hand. I tried to tune out the verbal taunts, and focused on getting from one class to the next.

After graduation

The negative effects of bullying can intensify for years or decades after leaving the abuse (Jantzer, 2006). I can attest to this because it was my experience as well. My college career began in a community college only a few miles from home. It was a different town but some of the people I went to high school were there. Thankfully, they were a minority and I was able to avoid them most of the time. I got a part-time job at a grocery store and started making friends. As I began coming out of my shell, I also began the process of discovering who I was.

I kept telling myself that the bullying was over but I still reacted as if the bullying was a part of my life. If a can of food hit the floor at the grocery store or there was another loud noise, I ducked or cringed. Several of my co-workers noticed my over-reactions but didn't say anything. I was always on edge and felt like everyone was a potential bully. The anger that I had swallowed for all those years came out in the middle of minor confrontations. I got into it with one supervisor over mopping the floors properly and nearly lost my job. It seemed I was constantly in conflict with someone at work or school. I carried a perpetual chip on my shoulder and my attitude dared anyone to knock that chip off.

That job at the grocery store led to my first date during my sophomore year of college. Tammi was a sweet girl who worked in the deli area at the same grocery store as I did. She was eighteen and one of my friends at the grocery store noticed her flirting with me. I told him he was crazy but I noticed she kept smiling at me and appeared to find reasons to talk to me. I was so scared of being rejected again that it took me two months to ask her out. When she said yes, I almost asked her to repeat her answer. I couldn't believe she actually wanted to go out with me. On our second date I kissed her, and to my utter amazement she kissed me back. My attempt was very awkward but Tammi didn't seem to care. She was patient with me, and over the next couple of months taught me how to kiss a woman and tried to show me what it meant to be in a relationship.

The problem came when she left for college that fall. She wanted to go without the strings of a relationship back home, so she broke up with me. I was devastated. It wasn't just the end of the relationship. I took it much further. The rejection from girls in high school came crashing in on me. I could hear their laughter and I again felt like I was destined to be alone. All sense of perspective was gone. I sulked at work and school and pushed everyone away from me.

I buried that pain and added it to the pain and bitterness

I nursed to keep me going. I graduated from Wabash Valley Community College with a C average and managed to get admitted into Southern Illinois University. As I prepared to live away from home for the first time, I bounced between hope for a brighter future and dread of more social situations. Could I make friends like I did in junior college? I still didn't know what to major in but I chose business. I figured it was the fastest way to make money and show those who had hurt me that I was better than they were.

New environment - same issues

My first day at the dorm I met Ed from Chicago. We hit it off and I started feeling like I could make friends and be successful. Ed introduced me to his group of friends and before long I had a group of friends of my own. However, I lost many of them by the end of the first semester. The rage and bitterness inside came out, especially if I drank much at all. I started several fights in bars and many of my friends stopped inviting me to go out with them. The rejection convinced me to stop drinking and I started getting invited out again. But the rage was always there. I would scream at people for minor offenses and walked around like a pit bull with a bad attitude.

It came to a head on Halloween night 1986. I went out with a group of friends to the big block party. SIU always had a massive Halloween party. College students from all over the country came to Carbondale for this party. I got into an argument with a friend who was totally wasted. The rage swelled and I had to hit something. I didn't want to hit my friend because he was too drunk to realize what he was saying. So I hit a brick wall.

I spent several hours in the emergency room getting X-rays. I had broken two knuckles. While most of my friends were partying and having a good time, I was sitting in the

emergency room. It wasn't the first time that I had hurt my-self in an attempt to drown the pain. It should have made me change but instead I added it to the self-loathing I was carry-ing around with me.

I was also struggling in the classroom. Business wasn't what I wanted to do and the anger wasn't enough to keep me motivated. Most days I skipped class and hung out with friends. However, my circle of friends was getting thin. I flunked the fall semester, and withdrew from the university half-way through the spring semester.

For the next five years, my life continued to spiral out of control. I lived in Chicago for a couple of years and had sev-eral friends. However, I struggled to keep the rage down. It was eating me up inside. The rage combined with low self-es-teem and self-loathing made me feel like I didn't belong any-where. I blamed my constant confrontations at work on the other people I was having issues with. After two years at the same job, I had started to see everyone as a potential enemy. I found a job closer to home and moved back in with my par-ents. But the company went out of business, leaving me un-employed.

In desperation, I enlisted in the Air Force. Half-way through basic training I pulled a muscle in my back. They offered to let me go back to the first day of training and start over or go home on a medical discharge. I wasn't fitting in well in the military, so I decided to take the chance to get out. When I went home, I felt like I had failed again. The failures at SIU and the Air Force threatened to pull me down in the depths of such a deep depression that I was afraid I would never come out of it.

A few months after returning home from the Air Force, I hit rock bottom. My parents and I were not getting along well because they were frustrated that I would never stick to anything long enough to finish it. I moved out of my parents'

house and into a rented room of a large home. The owners rented rooms to men on a weekly basis. There was no kitchen and a shared bathroom. I was working a seasonal part-time job at K-mart and barely making ends meet. I had also racked up a few thousand dollars in credit card debt and had no way to repay it.

When I got laid off from my job at K-mart, I only had enough money for one week of rent and a couple of days of food. I didn't qualify for unemployment, because I was only working part time. All my failures were crashing in on me and I decided to end the torment. The biggest struggle I had wasn't the thought of suicide itself. In fact, the thought of not being alive, and not having to deal with the pain, was comforting. I was struggling with how to somehow get it through to my parents that it wasn't their fault. My heart ached knowing that I was about to hurt them terribly but I couldn't stand the thought of a future full of nothing but rejection, failure and loneliness.

I didn't want to die, but I didn't want to live like this anymore. The vision of getting evicted and living on the street with no hope filled my mind, and I could see even more physical and mental abuse being hurled at me as a homeless man in a small town. I couldn't take it anymore. The fear of the afterlife haunted me. What if there really was a hell? I was living in hell and I didn't want to go from one form of hell to another. That thought taunted me but it paled in comparison to the pain that was eating me up inside. I planned to write a letter to my parents, take an entire bottle of sleeping pills and finally get some relief from the pain.

I went to the little diner down the street and ordered a burger. It seemed like a strange dish for a last meal, but it was all I could afford. As I sat there alone, I watched families laughing and smiling. They seemed to be living in an entirely different reality. I wanted desperately to have someone to love and a family of my own but I knew it would never happen for me. The burger seemed to rot in my mouth. I choked that first bite down and pushed it away.

A new beginning

There is often a catalyst that seems to jump start change in a person's life. It can be the death of a loved one, the support of a friend, the love of a romantic partner or any other major life event. In my case, it was a religious experience that initiated the process.

As I walked out of the diner, I was surprisingly calm. I decided to check to see if I had any phone messages. There was a message from Bob, one of my mom's friends. He was asking me if I wanted to go to church with them the next night. To this day I don't know why I agreed to go, but I decided one more day wasn't going to make that much of a difference.

Thursday night a group of my mom's friends picked me up and we headed to church. I watched as the power lines passed by the car in slow motion, and listened to the group talking about their jobs and their families. I was so lost in my thoughts that I didn't notice that we had pulled into the parking lot of the church. I was thinking about was the sweet silence from the taunting voices of the bullies and my own failures that death would bring. Nobody else in the car knew what thoughts were filling my mind, and I felt at peace about it. Nobody seemed to notice anything out of the ordinary.

As we entered the church the singing started. I just stood there and mouthed the words. In the middle of the second song a nagging thought kept running through my mind. I tried to think of anything else but it wouldn't go away. I heard, "You have tried everything else and it has all failed. Give me a chance." As the song ended, the pastor did something strange. He stepped up to the microphone, and asked

the music director to pause before starting the next song. The pastor said he felt that God was speaking to someone there. He wasn't sure what the exact words were, but it was close to "You have tried everything but nothing has worked" and that "God wants you to give Him a chance." He stated the altar was open if anyone wanted to give God that chance. It was almost word for word what I was hearing in my thoughts and I felt a huge knot in my stomach. I was shaking as I walked to the front of the church. It had been years since I cried. There were many times that I screamed in anger but there were no tears. I wanted the release from tears, but the pain was buried too deeply. The tears wouldn't flow. The only emotion I seemed to be able to express was anger and I was quite skilled at expressing it.

As I fell to my knees at that altar the tears wouldn't stop. I'm not sure how long I was there, but when I finally raised my head my shirt was soaked in tears. There were several people around me praying for me. They handed me a box of tissue and helped me to my feet. The rest of that night is a blur, but I know I felt lighter. The mild euphoria remained for the next couple of days, and I decided I wouldn't end my life.

One of the people there gave me a little cash to get some food. I hadn't said anything about being broke, but he had heard from my mom that I had been laid off. It was enough to pay the next week's rent and eat for another week or so.

A few days after that church service I was told about a temporary job at a local factory. The pay wasn't great and it didn't have benefits. But it was stable employment. I started the job the next week and was able to continue living in the rented room. After a few weeks I was able to start paying my bills off. My parents heard from a friend that she had seen me and that I seemed to be changing my attitude. They offered to let me move back home for a while to get back on my feet.

Moving back home after I had failed so often was incredibly humbling. Instead of fighting it, however, I looked at it as a fresh start.

The factory I was working at was also a chance for another fresh start. None of the people there knew me or anything about my past. It didn't take long for me to start making friends. I worked hard at controlling my rage, but quickly realized something had happened that night at the altar. The release from the tears had opened the floodgates. Instead of swallowing the pain and pushing it down with anger, I let the tears flow when nobody was around. As I allowed myself to start feeling the pain rather than fighting it, part of my rage subsided.

Over the next two years I started learning how to forgive and discovered healthier ways of dealing with life. I didn't have the money to hire a professional counselor, but I had access to a library. In my search for a better way of dealing with life, I read every self-help book I could get my hands on and listened to audio tapes on my forty-five minute drive to and from work. I studied works by Dale Carnegie, Dr. Norman Vincent Peale, Joel Osteen, Tony Robbins and many others. I was desperate to find healing and a better way of approaching life.

Going back to SIU

The lessons I learned from those books and tapes, and from my own successes and failures, enabled me build a better foundation for living. That foundation was in place when the factory laid me off a year and a half later. I was ready to go back and rebuild my life and I had taken time to think about what I wanted to do. I wasn't sure what my long-term career choice was but I knew I needed to finish the education I had started at SIU. As I considered what I was passionate about, reading and writing kept coming up over and over again. I wasn't sure what I wanted to do with it, but I decided to enroll in the English program. At the end of the first semester I had a 3.5 average and I knew that my life had finally started to go in a better direction. I ran out of financial aid and had to work full-time and attend school part-time, but after another three years I finally finished my bachelor's degree.

Shortly after I finished my bachelor's degree, I got a job at the university's law library. One of the benefits was free tuition. That position allowed me to take classes part time and complete my master's degree in Mass Communication and Media Arts.

It took much longer for me to learn how to have more healthy romantic relationships. A few months after returning to Southern Illinois University, I met a woman who was interested in me. A part of me was still very insecure when it came to women. She used humor and verbal put downs as a way of showing affection. However, that humor was often masking some pretty hurtful comments. I grabbed on quickly to the affection, despite the often hurtful comments. We married six months after we met.

We were married for fifteen years. As the marriage became more and more rocky the insults became more cutting, and sugar coating with humor couldn't keep me from feeling the sting. I still felt unworthy of love, so I put up with the verbal put downs. To this day, I still don't think she realized how mean a lot of her comments were. She was dealing with her own issues from the past and unintentionally projecting a portion of that anger towards me. I even started laughing at the insults as a way of being part of the fun. However, it wasn't always fun. Many of the words were hurtful, but I thought it was normal. It wasn't until I was in counseling during the divorce that I discovered how abusive the insults were

A radically changed life

I'm remarried now and my wife, Tina, builds me up instead of cutting me down. It is wonderful to have someone in my life who believes in me and supports me in my career and social life. She shows me love and affection freely with no strings attached. In fact, Tina has gently pushed me to write this book and get it published. She believes in me more than I do.

I make most of my living doing a combination of graphic design, photography and teaching. My circle of friends is large and supportive. We often get together in groups to hang out, laugh and enjoy life. My son, Joel, is doing well, despite his struggles with Asperger's (a form of autism).

Life isn't perfect, and there are tough times. In the past ten years, I've been through a divorce and custody battle, lost my dad, had periods of unemployment, and tried to be there for Tina through the death of her father. There are still times that I struggle with issues from the past. But those struggles are much less frequent or severe.

Near the end of my master's program, I had the opportunity to see a professional counselor who helped me deal with the few issues that remained. I saw a second counselor during the divorce process. Both of these counselors helped me learn to stop the obsessing about the past and look at situations from a more realistic and positive perspective. As I thought about what I wanted to do after getting out of school, I started feeling a deep desire to help other adults who were bullied and still struggling with low self-esteem, anger, anxiety and depression. At that time, there had been studies done on bullying in school but there was little out there to show the long-term effects of bullying. This desire to help other victims find healing birthed an interest in reading about psychology.

I also discovered the relatively new field of positive psychology. Martin Seligman's book *Learned Optimism: How to Change Your Mind and Your Life* was vital in helping me solidify what I had been endeavoring to implement in my life. His book showed me how to focus on the positive things I wanted out of life rather than the negatives.

As bullying has garnered more attention, researchers have devoted more time to studying bullying, including its long-term effects. As I read about these studies, I found that I wasn't alone. Many victims struggle with depression, low self-esteem, substance abuse and anxiety disorders as adults (Sourander and Jensen, 2007). This research validated my own struggles, and struggles of others I've met, with depression, anxiety, anger and low self-esteem long after leaving high school.

The remainder of this book will be focused on the long term effects of bullying, some ineffective coping mechanisms and ways to begin the process of healing. You may see yourself in much of this book. It may become apparent that many of your struggles as an adult are related to the abuse you suffered at the hands of the bullies. You will also find a roadmap to show you how to start healing, not just coping. You may still need professional counseling to deal with the pain and anger that you carry, but the strategies in this book will help you get started on the right path.

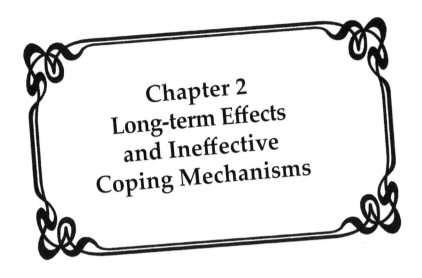

Chapter 2
Long-term Effects and Ineffective Coping Mechanisms

The trauma from the bullying didn't end when you left middle school and/or high school. There was damage to your psyche, and you likely adopted ineffective and possibly self-destructive ways of coping with the pain and anger. The following chapters will introduce you to some ways that psychological damage can affect your personality. There will be explanations of several negative coping mechanisms that can keep you from having the level of success in your career and relationships you desire.

These chapters are presented as personas that I've observed in other victims and struggled with myself. These personas include the Underachiever, Overachiever, People Pleaser and Punisher

Each of these personas is a result of the anger, anxiety and damage to the self-esteem that bullying inflicted on you. There is also a chapter summarizing additional negative coping mechanisms including overeating, sexual addiction, imagination and drugs and/or alcohol.

Some of these personas and ineffective coping mechanisms will resonate with you more than others. You likely adopted more than one negative coping mechanism to varying degrees. Your personality is multi-faceted and you had to develop more than one way to cope with the trauma.

There is a possibility as you delve into these issues you could be tempted to use them as an excuse to continue the behaviors and attitudes that are preventing you from reaching your potential in your career and having meaningful relationships. Another possibility is seeing one or more of these negative coping mechanisms in yourself and feeling like you are doomed to stay where you are forever. However, I want to state clearly that you can overcome the bullying and any ineffective skills you developed to survive. You can be free of the anger, self-loathing, depression, anxiety and feelings of loss that can stem from the bullying.

At the root of many of the long-term issues related to bullying are low self-esteem and anger (Carlisle and Rofes, 2007). These emotions can affect how you deal with your peers at work, your family and friends.

If you experienced physical abuse, it can take years to overcome. However, it is often the mental and verbal abuse that takes the bigger toll. The over-arching message pounded into you was that you are worthless or less valuable than your peers. No matter how much you tried to not let it affect you, you likely internalized the feelings of worthlessness (Vanderbilt and Augustyn, 2010).

Those feelings are like an emotional cancer. You can look normal on the outside, but inside you struggle to feel like you have any real value. You know it isn't true, but part of you may still feel like there was something wrong with you that made the bullies target you. How can you possibly be successful in dealing with others, when you feel inferior to everyone else?

The anger is another weight you likely carry from the bullying. You couldn't fight back effectively during the bullying, so you had to keep pushing the anger deeper and deeper. A part of you may still have a great deal of resentment and bitterness towards the bullies for the abuse they inflicted on you. You might even be angry at yourself for not finding a way to stop the bullying.

That anger is a constant companion that metastasizes and transforms into bitterness. It can push anyone away who tries to get close. How can you trust anyone enough to get close after you were abused by your peers? Your bitterness can become a wall that protects you from getting hurt, but also keeps you from receiving love and friendship. Inside that protective barrier you feel alone and empty.

The combination of anger and self-loathing can be incredibly toxic. The anger towards the bullies can be projected towards anyone who you have a very minor conflict with. You might exhibit outward signs of anger such as using aggressive language or physical intimidation, or you might emotionally shut down and refuse to deal with conflict. Either response will push others away from you, while preventing you from growing as a person.

Anxiety, especially social anxiety, is one other common long-term effect of bullying. You may have become fearful of crowds and social situations because you were humiliated and/or tortured. The leaders might have used social power and clout to get other students to become bullies to avoid being targets themselves. You were then facing a group of bullies rather than only one person. It is only natural that you would possibly connect social situations with the bullying and trauma.

If you are struggling with issues related to anger and self-loathing from the bullying, you are not alone. A study from King's College London concluded that,

> ...adults who were bullied as kids suffered from suicidal thoughts and other psychological disorders at

higher rates than folks who weren't bullied. Those who were bullied were also in poorer shape, performed worse on intelligence tests, struggled with higher rates of unemployment and lower pay, and were less likely to be in a romantic relationship (Heid, 2014).

This may validate your own struggles to find success in your career and form deep, meaningful relationships with other people. The bullying likely kept you stuck in the past.

As you read the next few chapters describing personas and negative coping mechanisms, ask yourself which ones part of your life. Have they cost you success in your career or relationships?

Section 2
Negative Coping
Mechanisms

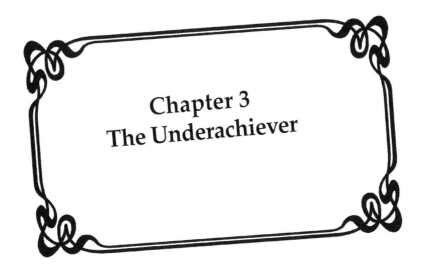

Chapter 3
The Underachiever

The Underachiever could be described succinctly in one simple phrase: "unfulfilled potential." Have you ever felt that you have a lot of potential, but your lack of confidence, anger or other issues from the bullying have kept you from reaching that potential? Do you often refrain from opportunities to test your abilities or take on projects that could showcase your abilities? Are you ever scared to approach potential romantic partners because of feelings of inferiority or fear of being rejected?

After leaving high school, you likely wanted to make a fresh start in college or the workforce. However, you entered this new environment with a huge disadvantage. Your self-image was likely severely damaged. You might have made a conscious decision to leave the past behind and start fresh, but you can't escape yourself and the pain you carry. If you don't get help dealing with the pain and low self-esteem, it will show in your relationships with others. Your low self-esteem and anger have likely hindered your academic or workplace performance and will continue to hinder your career growth.

You live in a world where fitting into the social constructs is required to prosper. A large part of fitting in is how you communicate with those around you. This communication consists of much more than the words you use in conversations. Less than half of communication is verbal. The rest is non-verbal communication including eye contact, facial expressions, body movements, and tone of voice.

You can say one thing, but if your feelings don't match your words or you are trying to hide information, the non-verbal cues betray the true meaning behind the spoken words. Think back to your interactions with others. Do you ever remember a situation where a friend or relative said yes but their body language said no?

This was often the case when you were a victim of bullying. The verbal taunts and derogatory remarks made you feel less valuable than your peers and it likely still shows in your non-verbal cues. For example, you might not look people in the eyes with confidence. If a classmate or co-worker does make eye contact, you may quickly lower your eyes. Maintaining eye contact with another person requires real confidence.

Many non-verbal cues are out of your control. You can temporarily think consciously about how you hold your body, but it is hard to maintain a false bravado for any length of time. For example, when you first meet a potential employer for an interview you can make a conscious effort to stand straight and tall, hold your shoulders square, give a firm handshake and make eye contact. By the end of the interview, however, you may catch yourself slumping in the chair or not making eye contact. As the questions continue and the tension builds, you may sit with your arms crossed or another closed off position. It's a subconscious attempt to protect yourself from being hurt and rejected. Unfortunately, these same non-verbal cues can signal the potential employer that you are not a good fit for the company or that you don't feel confident enough in your skills to perform well in the position.

College life

Watch a group of college students standing together; it is very easy to see who is confident and who isn't. Some students seem to feel at ease in their own skin. They stand in a relaxed pose, but their shoulders and back are held strong without effort. They hold their heads high and easily make eye contact with every person in the group. The leaders of the group will often hold eye contact with the weaker willed student until he or she breaks eye contact. This is especially true with men who use this to establish themselves as the alpha-male in the group.

The less confident people in the group are polar opposites from the leaders. They look awkward. Their shoulders are slumped and they struggle to make and maintain eye contact. They often hang their head low or look down at the ground. Instead of using their hands effectively as they talk, they fidget nervously, bite their nails or hold their arms crossed to keep from fidgeting. Their voices are low and soft and they will often stutter or stumble to get their words out. They may not speak at all and look for the first opportunity to get away from the social situation, even avoiding social gatherings altogether. If another student does drag them to a party, they might end up in a corner by themselves.

Despite the low self-esteem that causes interpersonal issues in college, many adult victims of bullying thrive academically. On paper they seem to be successful. Researching and writing papers are by their very nature solitary pursuits. Even the sciences are solitary, requiring many hours alone or in a small group in a lab. Additionally, these students can use the mental effort required as an escape. They spend so much mental energy studying and researching that they can push their underlying issues aside. This can further enhance the illusion that they are emotionally healthy and successful. They may win awards for their academic achievements or go for a doctorate and become experts in their fields. They may appear confident when speaking about their expertise but are awkward in more general conversations. I have met many professors who fit this mold. Academia tolerates a lot of quirks and odd behavior as long as the professor or researcher continues to get published and his or her behavior isn't overly offensive to students or colleagues.

Other past victims, however, do not fare well in college. Their underlying low self-esteem causes them to sabotage any possibility of success. They subconsciously feel like they are failures, so they do things to ensure their performance matches their self-image. They might take too many hours to complete projects or question every word on a paper, which dooms them to failure. Another strong possibility is procrastination. They don't think they are smart enough to understand the material. So, out of fear, they put off studying. Eventually, deadlines force them to tackle the work, but they leave themselves without adequate time to complete the assignment.

The workplace

The damage from the bullying becomes much more evident in the workplace. Even if you managed to have a successful academic career, you are likely to struggle as you make the transition from college to the world of work. It begins with the job search, which resembles a field full of land mines. You are so scared of stepping on a land mine that you stand still. Your fear keeps you from moving forward. Your low self-esteem prevents you from even considering some positions. You may assume that there are lots of people that are more qualified than you. This can cause you to only apply for jobs that you are over-qualified for.

After you apply, you have to interview for the position. Interviewing requires confidence, and the ability to sell yourself and your abilities to a potential employer. Once on the job, you may perform your duties well but struggle socially within the corporate environment. You can become a victim of bullying in the workplace. One study stated:

> We found a significant relationship between reported roles in school bullying, and experience of workplace victimization. The highest risk of workplace victimization was for those who were both bullies and victims at school, followed by those who were only victims (Smith, Singer, Monika, Helge & Cary, 2003).

People might take advantage of you, taking credit for your work. You may not tout your achievements and get passed over for promotions. You can be especially vulnerable to unscrupulous managers who may take your ideas and present them as their own. These same managers will use poor performance reviews to reinforce your negative self-image and keep you from moving up in the company. If you are seen as competition or as an obstacle to the manager's advancement, the manager may find a reason to fire you or make the environment hostile enough that you quit. Your underlying self-image can make it difficult to find the confidence and courage to fight to keep your position.

Every time you are passed up for a promotion or lose a job, you may assume it's your fault and view it as a failure. Each incident reinforces your low self-image, and makes you feel that you are not worthy of obtaining and keeping a good job. This can easily reinforce the cycle of failure and self-loathing that began during the bullying. A look at your resume may reveal either chronic underachievement or job hopping.

Relationships

Careers aren't the only area where low self-esteem may make it difficult for you to succeed. You may also struggle in relationships, especially romantic relationships. How can you possibly have a healthy, loving relationship with another person if you hate yourself or feel that you are unworthy of love?

There are three primary ways that you can sabotage romantic relationships or the opportunity to develop these relationships. These include smothering a romantic partner, avoidance and anger.

The first stems directly from your deep desire for love and acceptance. When someone shows you affection, you become a sponge. You soak up the affection and smother the object of that affection. Any attempt by your significant other to get needed space is seen as a rejection. Feeling rejected again, you may attempt to pull them even closer. Eventually, the partner has no choice but to end the relationship. You find yourself questioning what you did wrong. After all, you gave your time, your financial resources and your affection. The more you gave to your partner, the more he/she pulled away. It doesn't make sense from your perspective.

This can start another vicious cycle. When you go into the next romantic relationship, you may try harder to get close. If you go down this road, every relationship can end more quickly than the one before. Your desire to give of yourself and get emotionally close can be very attractive at the beginning of a relationship. Everyone wants to feel special and your willingness to give freely and show affection does that. The object of that affection feels that he or she is special and loved because another person loves them so passionately. However, this obsessive need to be emotionally and physically connected pushes them away ever more quickly. You might be able to look back at a string of broken relationships that looks like a train derailed.

Another pitfall that may cause you to fail at romantic relationships is avoiding them altogether. You may never approach a potential partner. If you are a man, you may never get the nerve up to ask a woman out. If you are a woman who was a victim of bullying, you may make excuses any time a man asks you out.

You may assume that the man is only after sex, because no man would want you for the person you are on the inside. Here again, every interaction with another person ends in failure and reinforces your belief that you are unworthy of love.

In order to get into a romantic relationship, you have to go where people are and interact with others. If your self-image is negative and you feel less valuable than your peers, you may avoid social situations where meeting a potential mate becomes a possibility. When you occasionally find yourself at a party or club, you end up sitting in a corner alone rather than mingling with others. You are surrounded by people, yet feel utterly alone. No matter how much you might want to meet others, your body language likely tells others to leave you alone. You may feel conflicted. Part of you wants anyone to come up to you and start a conversation, but another part of you fears you can't make small talk and will end up blowing the opportunity to be social with your peers.

One last way you might sabotage romantic relationships is with anger or rage. You may be able to suppress anger from the bullying in normal day to day interactions. However, it's much harder to hide in a more intimate relationship. It may show up either physically or verbally. A simple confrontation can bring up anger from the past and your overly aggressive reaction to the situation will do permanent damage to the relationship. The aggression may be forgiven the first couple of

times it surfaces, but a healthy partner will not put up with rage when they see it as a pattern of behavior.

If you do end up in a long-term relationship, it may not be a healthy one. You might end up with a person who uses your low self-esteem to their advantage. The partner might be controlling and use that control to dominate you. This sets up a long-term abuser and victim relationship. You put up with being controlled or abused because part of you feels it is normal. The longer you remain in the relationship, the more normal it seems. This abuse, whether verbal or physical, validates your distorted and damaged self-image.

You might find a partner who also has low self-esteem or other similar issues themselves. If so, there is a strong possibility that the two of you will end up in a co-dependent relationship in which neither partner is growing or attempting to overcome their emotional issues. In fact, you can reinforce negative behaviors while covering for them in public. Possible issues that may be occurring inside the relationship but look normal on the outside include alcohol or prescription drug abuse, depression, sexual abuse or a sustained victim mentality on the part of one or both of you.

It can become the two of you versus a cruel world that is intent on keeping you down. You aren't forced to deal with the underlying issues because you can always go home and tell your partner how a particular person refused to hire you, promote you or include you in social situations because they have something against you. Instead of taking a realistic look at the situation and evaluating both your side of the story and the other person's side, the co-dependent partner coddles you and reinforces the view that everything is someone else's fault.

Other than a possible co-dependent relationship, the failures in your professional life and romantic life continually reinforce your feelings of worthlessness. If nothing is done,

you may end up deeply depressed, alone and broke. The unresolved issues from your past can destroy your life.

You might manage to find a job where you get by without having to deal with your issues. If you become comfortable enough, you can bury yourself in the work and have a modicum of success. However, you may avoid moving up the ladder, when the opportunity is presented. Your career could best be described as unrealized potential. You could accomplish so much if you could get past the issues from the past abuse. Friends and family might tell you that you would be a perfect catch and they can't understand why you aren't able to get involved in a stable romantic relationship. Here again, you could have much more if you could just get past the trauma and low self-esteem from the bullying.

The third section of the book will show you how to begin the process of healing and how to get started on a path to a more fulfilling life. Many of these steps will be uncomfortable because they will mean dealing with the bullying and the trauma from that abuse. I promise you, there is hope. My life is now full of love, friendship, and success. I still occasionally struggle with the past, but these struggles are less severe and less frequent with time.

You can have a bright future and healing from the bullying.

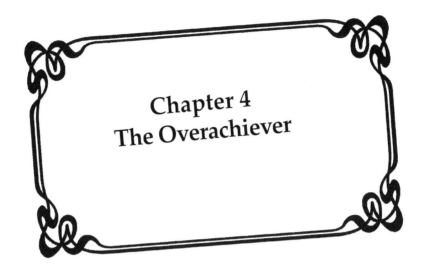

Chapter 4
The Overachiever

The Overachiever appears to be the polar opposite of the underachiever. The overachiever is driven to constantly achieve more in academic or work environments. Being ambitious is normally a good thing, but an overachiever often lacks balance. He or she puts in too many hours or becomes so obsessed with achieving the next level in his/her career that there is little time or energy left for family or friends.

The surprising thing is that for former victims of bullying, the explanation for the lack of balance and accompanying issues is often the same for both the underachiever and overachiever. Low self-esteem was the primary explanation for underachiever, and the reason why many former victims do not achieve all that they are capable of in their career and personal lives. That same low self-esteem can push you to constantly need to achieve more yet never feel like you have accomplished enough. Jodee Blanco, the author of Please Stop Laughing at Me: One Woman's Inspirational True Story, addressed this on her website. She stated that "Perhaps, [sic] you've become an overachiever like me, driving yourself into the ground because the only way you can turn off those old voices from school is to keep trying to drown them out with accomplishment" (Blanco, 2013).

You likely developed several coping mechanisms to survive the bullying while it was happening. But what do you do after you get away from the abuse? During the bullying, you didn't have anyone to come to your aid and stop it. You might have had a few close friends you confided in but most likely you suffered alone and in silence. After leaving school and the bullies behind, you were left to your own devices to find a way to cope with the damage to your self-esteem as you tried to create a new life.

Leaving high school and entering college or the workforce is a daunting task for everyone. However, the bullying you suffered likely presented additional challenges. When you have been abused by your peers for a long period of time, you not only have a negative self-image; you have a constant fear of not being good enough to be accepted by those around you. This makes the thought of entering college or the workforce more intimidating. As you enter college or the workforce, a part of you looks optimistically towards this as a fresh start. Your peers in the new environment don't know your past and were not part of the culture where the abuse occurred. You left that culture, and the bullies, behind.

Another part of your psyche, however, fears having to face the challenges of meeting new people and fitting into a new culture when you may feel that your social skills are insufficient. How could you develop the social skills needed to enter this new environment when you were doing your best to survive? You fear that you will fail again to fit in and make friends, and possibly be victimized again.

The façade

One way of coping with this fear and anxiety is to cover

it up. If you are an overachiever, you put on a façade of confidence and create an alter ego. You can observe people that are confident and successful. You imitate these successful people's mannerisms and the way they perform academically or on their job. Even if you have very little natural acting ability, you can fake it till you make it.

You can test these skills in social circles where part of the people know you. The response of these friends, family members or coworkers allow you to gauge how effective these new skills are. You take mental notes on what worked and what didn't, and make the appropriate modifications. The language can be learned quickly, but mastering the body language and other non-verbal communications skills may take much more time. With concentrated effort, however, you can master these skills.

Every time you get a positive reaction from others, you replicate that behavior. Each success breeds more success and a part of you may legitimately become more confident. For example, Jodee Blanco, who wrote the book Stop Laughing at Me, became confident in her ability to communicate in the business world. She eventually became a successful publicist and worked with celebrities from all over the world. Yet she found herself in a parking lot paralyzed with fear at the thought of attending her high school reunion and seeing the bullies again.

It is possible that you used your new persona to get a quality husband or wife, a great career and have what most would consider a nearly perfect life. By developing a measure of self-confidence and beginning to create a successful career and family life, you can avoid having to face your low self-esteem from the bullying. If you buried it, the success is only a shell. However, you likely still struggle inside with self-doubt and loathing. The effort required to maintain the façade can be exhausting.

House of cards

A major crisis such as a death of a parent, divorce or job loss can cause that shell to collapse. When you are forced to face the pain and anger from the bullying, it will come out of left field to those around you. Most of these people didn't know you when the abuse was happening. Your friends, your spouse and children may not understand why you're falling apart. Don't be afraid to share with those close to you what you went through. Getting the issues out in the open and asking for help are critical steps in overcoming the abuse you suffered.

In college or the workforce, you can throw yourself completely into your work. The activity serves as an escape from the pain inside. It is easier to focus your energy into whatever project you are working on rather than dealing with issues from the past. Work becomes an escape and can become all consuming.

Although focusing your creativity, energy and effort into your career can bring success, it can also make relationships difficult to maintain. People are attracted to your success, but quickly realize you are not the person you pretend to be in public. It can lead to a string of failed friendships and romantic relationships.

Unfortunately, this can start a downward spiral that is every bit as damaging as that of an underachiever. Success at work and failures in your personal life encourage you to further focus on work. Every failure means more hours at work and leaves less time to socialize or develop meaningful relationships. Many executives are working longer hours than ever before. The longer hours are ". . . wreaking havoc on private lives and taking a toll on health and well-being" (Hewlett and Luce, 2006).

This spiral can have many detrimental effects. The most

common issue is burnout. This can be emotional, physical or both. Your long hours at work take their toll and your mind and/or body shut down. Depending on the severity of the burnout, you might lose the money and success you have gained. You can spend years creating a successful career but it can come crashing down in a very short period of time. This can force you to confront the underlying issues from your past in a very traumatic fashion. Now you have to deal with failure in your career and the trauma from the bullying all at once.

You can manage to stave off burnout for a while, but you will likely face another crisis farther down the road. If you have maintained your vigilance at work and climbed the ladder of success, you may be the envy of many of your colleagues. However, you will eventually retire. Putting in too many hours at work results in not having developed many meaningful friendships or romantic relationships. You might have left behind a string of broken relationships as you climbed the corporate ladder. Now you are suddenly faced with no work to do and no one to share your life with. The end result is the same as burnout. You are forced to deal with your past if you want any chance at a meaningful life after retirement.

There is, however, a bigger underlying issue. No matter how much you achieve, if you have self-esteem issues from the bullying you may never feel accepted or valued as a person. You are attempting to gain self-worth from external success. It may work for a while but this success proves hollow. Look at the rich and famous people who have committed suicide or destroyed their lives with drugs and alcohol. Some examples include Whitney Houston, Anna Nicole Smith, Michael Jackson, Elvis Presley and John Belushi. No amount of success can bring true happiness if you don't like yourself.

Your need to be validated by external success can also

push you to achieve more. If you are able to prevent burnout you are likely stressed most of the time. You're like an old fashioned watch that's been wound too tightly or a rubber band stretched too thin. You often seem to be on the edge of an explosion of anger or a nervous breakdown. This can push you towards perfectionism. Any minor error is seen as a complete failure and you badger yourself emotionally.

As a result of this need for external validation, you may take on too many projects. You're danger of taking on more than any one person can accomplish. You get stretched so thin that you fail to prioritize and don't complete major projects. You might prioritize well enough to get the biggest projects done, but not the smaller projects. In that case, your superiors may be impressed with your performance, but you will not be satisfied with your performance and inwardly feel like a failure. This will further entrench the self-loathing that you work hard to hide from everyone around you.

Unreasonable demands on others

Your need to constantly push yourself and your colleagues harder pushes co-workers away. As you climb the ladder of success, you will have to supervise others. Your perfectionism and overzealous drive to achieve is often projected onto those under you. You also expect your subordinates to put in the same hours and commitment to the job. You may not empathize with the fact that many of the people under you have families and lives outside of work. Your subordinates may quickly become frustrated by the unreasonable demands you place on them. These employees either quit, attempt to fight back or simply meet the bare minimum requirements for their jobs. The morale of the department can deteriorate quickly and production may fall sharply.

If too many employees quit, or you have hostile work environment charges filed, upper management will put pressure on you to smooth things over. You can feign concern for your subordinates but it is only surface. Inwardly, you often end up despising their apparent lack of commitment to the job. Most people can sense if a person genuinely cares about them, and they resent a manager that doesn't truly value them as individuals. As you climb the ladder, you may leave behind groups of disgruntled employees.

Your unreasonable demands alienate your coworkers and create as many enemies as admirers. Many of these employees assume that you will fall in the future. They wait expectantly for you to tumble back down that ladder. If that happens, these disgruntled workers will revel in reminding you how far you've fallen. You have probably seen this happen to someone else who climbed the ladder quickly. Their failure, combined with the anger and vitriol from former employees, is enough to send them into a deep depression.

Working too many hours and not having a good balance of work and personal time can also lead to very serious health problems. According to Laura Wallace, manager of benefits for Arkansas Best Corporation, "Some of the health issues that can affect a workaholic might include higher stress levels, anger, depression and anxiety "(Smith, 2010). This can lead to high blood pressure, strokes or heart attacks.

The worst part of this façade that you as an overachiever maintain is that it can fool anyone who isn't close to you. You look like you are extremely successful. The people around you may never know how you are suffering inside. Similar to when you were experiencing the bullying, you suffer in silence. If you don't deal with the past, you will always feel empty inside and totally alone. Money or things can't fill that void or satisfy the need to connect with others.

Positive change can happen

There is hope. You can deal with the issues and regain a sense of balance. There is a good chance that you are in a solid position financially to pay for counseling, and you likely have not used much of the sick and personal time available to you. You can begin the process of healing while taking a small step back in your career. You can still be successful, but in a healthier manner. In the process, you can achieve closer relationships with your co-workers, family and friends.

You may find that you have been pursuing a career path that you have no genuine passion for. If you were focused on making lots of money or achieving a high status, you will discover how empty these pursuits are in and of themselves. You may begin looking at alternative careers where you can follow your passions. You may find the chapter on "Deciding on a Destination" particularly useful as you seek a new direction in your career.

If you choose to suddenly change your field or profession, be prepared for push back from those around you, especially if you are married. Changing your career path can lead to temporary financial difficulties that can be very frightening to your spouse and children who have become accustomed to a very affluent level of living. In the long run, however, these same family members will either come to value their closer relationship with you more than the money or choose to leave. You will need to discuss any plans with your family and together determine the best course of action.

If your family decides to leave, it is more evidence that you established these relationships based on the income you provided rather than true emotional connections. It will be tough, but finding that special person who loves you for who you are, not just what you can provide, is incredibly freeing and satisfying.

Chapter 5
The People Pleaser

The people pleaser, much like the under achiever and over achiever, is partially motivated by low self-esteem. The bigger motivation, however, is the fear of rejection. The bullies rejected you when you were at a very vulnerable point in your life. You know on a conscious level that you are worthy of love and acceptance, but a part of you might not believe it.

At SIU, I had a friend named Tony. He, like me, tried too hard to get people to like him. A look at a typical weekend for Tony will give a great mental picture of the life of a people pleaser.

It's late Friday night and Tony is baking cookies for the campus ministry bake sale in the morning. The phone rings. A friend, Allen, is too drunk to drive home. Allen calls Tony because he knows Tony will be there for him. Of course, Tony will be there; he can never say no. Tony quickly shuts the oven off, picks Allen up from the party and takes him home. Tony stays long enough to help Allen get to a bathroom and throw up without choking himself, washes him up a little bit and makes sure he is safely in bed. Getting back home around two in the morning, Tony still has to finish baking the cookies. But Tony's living in a shared house with other college students. They left a mess in the kitchen while he was out. Now Tony has to clean their mess before he can finish baking the cookies.

Tony crawls into bed at 3:30 am and gets up at 7:00 to get the cookies to the sale on time. While there, someone compliments Tony's cooking and asks him to help at another event at the church tomorrow. Tony knows he agreed to help Jennifer finish a major paper that's due Monday. If she doesn't get a great grade on this paper, her GPA might drop enough to keep her from getting into the graduate program she's been dreaming about.

Tony can't say no to the person in front of him. If he says no, they might not like him anymore. But he's wanted to go out with Jennifer for over a year now. If he helps Jennifer get a great grade on this paper, maybe she will finally agree to go out with him. Deep inside Tony knows better. Jennifer put him firmly in the friend zone a long time ago. She has cried on Tony's shoulder many times when other guys broke her heart. Every time she does this, Tony is screaming inside. He would treat Jennifer like a queen if she would only see him as more than just a nice guy.

It is late Saturday afternoon when Tony finishes the bake sale and breaks everything down. He practically runs home from the bake sale, gulps down a few bites of food and leaves to help Jennifer with her paper. She has a lot of work to finish and Tony knows it will be a long day. Around midnight Tony gets home and collapses on the bed, exhausted. The rough draft of the paper is close to being done.

At 7:00 am the alarm goes off. Tony rushes to church and helps with the event. Of course, he has to help clean up and get everything ready for next Sunday. Tony spends the rest of the afternoon and late into the evening writing and editing Jennifer's paper. Late Sunday night, he finally heads home.

As Tony starts to relax at home it suddenly hits him. Tony has a major paper due in the morning. He's been spending so much time helping everyone else that he forgot about the deadline in his own class. Tony's mind races as he grabs his computer and starts looking for research materials online.

Monday morning Tony stumbles into class with what he knows is a poorly written paper and only a couple of hours of sleep. He hears the voices of the bullies echoing in his ear that he's going to flunk this class and fail like he always does. The voices of the bullies continue to laugh and tell Tony that he is worthless and will never amount to anything. These same voices tell him that he'll flunk out of college and end up working at a dead end job with no friends or family to care for him. Visions of a future of loneliness and financial ruin fill Tony's mind, and he struggles not to weep as he hands in the paper and fights to stay awake enough to take notes in class.

An aerial view of Tony's life during his early college years would have resembled a Jackson Pollock painting with lines running everywhere on the canvas as he frantically ran from place to place trying to please everyone. Big splotches of paint would appear where he finally became so over-commit-ted that he started missing deadlines at work or school and couldn't fulfill all the promises he made socially. After burn-ing out, shutting down and becoming a big blob of paint for a little while, Tony would recover enough to start saying yes to everyone and the wild lines of paint would again begin streaking across the canvas until he shut down and another blob of paint appeared on the canvas. A part of Tony was scared that this pattern would continue until he was too old and exhausted to go any more. With no true friendships to fall back on, he'd die alone and utterly exhausted.

Like Tony, you want others to like you. You have unique abilities and talents that allow you to help others in ways nobody else can. You also have the universal equalizer,

limited time. There are only 24 hours in a day, and only so much that you can accomplish in that 24 hours. These common traits cause a lot of difficulty for you if you are a people pleaser.

The people pleaser's motivations

As a people pleaser, you are motivated by the same need for validation as the overachiever. The abuse inflicted during your school years leaves you feeling less valuable than others. Despite knowing the bullying wasn't your fault, on a much deeper level you might believe you're worthless. No matter what derogatory names or other abusive language the bullies used, the underlying message was that you are unworthy of friendship or love.

The bullying, and accompanying psychological damage, makes you more inclined to falli into the habit of people pleasing. It's tempting to seek acceptance and validation from others to compensate for the emptiness and rejection you endured during your formative years. If anyone shows you friendship or love, you may grab onto the hope that this person could be a good friend. The logic is if a special person cares for you, then you must be worthy of friendship and/or love.

The problem is that you may develop the false belief that you have to earn love and acceptance. You say yes to any request and often volunteer to help friends and co-workers with moving, work projects or anything that might earn brownie points.

Problems from people pleasing

Spending so much time trying to please others becomes a barrier to your own success. If you are spending all your time helping others, you won't have enough time or energy

to pursue your own dreams.

This is another area where my story can be a good example of developing ineffective life strategies to compensate for the pain and loneliness inflicted by bullying; I often exhausted myself helping everyone else. Despite the healing I've experienced, I still occasionally struggle with this issue. In my young adult years, I went from one extreme of anger and rage to capitulating to every request in a desperate attempt to feel valued and legitimized.

I was like a crack addict seeking my next fix. Every time someone thanked me or complimented me on my efforts, I felt a temporary high. For a short time I held my head high, but that external exhilaration couldn't change how I felt inside. The high quickly wore off and the self-loathing returned with a vengeance. It was similar to going shopping and purchasing something I really wanted. It made me happy for a short time, but as the new item became part of my routine, the good feelings faded.

As the good feelings from the praise of others faded, the negative feelings began to creep in. It usually started as feeling a little down. Then negative thoughts about my performance started to cross my mind. Since I was programmed by the bullies to focus on negatives about myself, I quickly grabbed onto a thought about anything I hadn't done well enough and began obsessing over it. I reviewed the perceived failure over and over again in my mind like a looping video clip.

It didn't take long for me to start looking for another chance to volunteer to help a person or organization in an attempt to recapture those good feelings. There are several problems with this but the biggest is that it was only an escape that allowed me to avoid dealing with the real problem, my low self-esteem.

The word missing from your vocabulary

You likely understand what I am talking about. The word "no" doesn't exist in your vocabulary. In addition to allowing you to avoid the underlying issues from the bullying, people pleasing can also cause burnout. As you take on more responsibility, you get stretched thin. Every waking moment is filled with other people's projects. You will sacrifice anything in order to keep juggling the different projects successfully, including sleep.

Nobody could keep up with all the projects that you take on. Eventually, you will run out of energy. Exhaustion and burnout are eminent.

Problems with relationships

Being a people pleaser can put a lot of pressure on a romantic relationship. Your spouse or significant other may feel like you are spending all of your time helping people. Things at home might not get done because you over committed to outside projects. So now there is pressure to get the outside projects done and pressure to spend more time dealing with life at home. This pressure accelerates the burnout process. It can cause the end of the romantic relationship. Nobody wants to feel like they are playing second fiddle to your other "friends." They may not understand why you're compelled to take on so many projects. He/she doesn't understand that you need praise from others to feel valued as a person.

Unfortunately, the burnout is not the end of the cycle. Similar to the overachiever, your work can come crumbling around you like a house of cards. You are forced to either stop all activity to give you mind and/or body time to recover, or cut down drastically on the number of projects you are working on.

As you are forced to take time to recover, you have to face the fact that you could not complete the projects you committed to. This means disappointing many of the people you promised to help. The healthy response would be to go to each of the people you committed to and tell them that you can't finish the projects. You could give each person the work that has been completed and ask forgiveness for not fulfilling your promise. However, this is not likely the way that you as a people pleaser will handle the situation.

Taking the initiative to contact the individuals who you committed to and asking to divulge yourself of the responsibilities takes a great deal of confidence. You need to have enough self-worth to know that your relationship with these people is strong enough to withstand the disappointment of not getting everything completed. If you had a healthier self-image, you would realize that if any of these "friends" break off the relationship they weren't true friends at all; they were users.

Attracting the wrong people

Unfortunately, as a people pleaser you will often attract people who are not interested in genuine friendship. You will attract people who want only what you can do for them. The relationship is great as long as you are doing lots of favors or providing professional services for free to the user. Once you cease to complete projects, the so-called "friend" ends the relationship. These users will often blame your lack of performance for ending the relationship, which makes you feel less worthy of true friendship.

Avoidance

Your low self-esteem makes it highly unlikely that you will

voluntarily let your friends know that you need to take a break from so many competing responsibilities. The more likely scenario is that you will attempt to avoid the individuals who you have committed to. You will not answer the phone or email.

You may go so far as to avoid certain stores, churches or any public place where you might run into one of the people you made commitments to. You may fear they will ask where you are on the project, and you will have to either lie about your progress, dodge the question or admit that you can't get the project done. Having to face these people can be devastating. You might withdraw from everyone and collapse into depression and self-loathing. The video of your past failures and the cruel taunts of the bullies may play over and over again in your mind. As each failure is replayed, it reinforces the message from the bullies.

You can't hide forever. You will have to face the people you promised to help. Some of these people will forgive you and the friendship will stay intact. Others, however, will end the relationship. The effects are made worse if you have avoided returning phone calls or emails from these individuals. The friendships that come to an end can cause a mixed bag of internal reactions. The ones who remain can be a boost to your self-esteem. The ones who choose to end the relationship, however, further reinforce your negative self-image.

Since your natural inclination is to focus on the negatives, you tend to focus on the relationships that ended and discount the reality that many people chose to remain friends. This does even more damage to your self-esteem.

As the fallout from not fulfilling your promises comes to a head, you will likely have one of two reactions. These include anger and doubling down on people pleasing. The first is to react with anger, assume they are all users and/or bullies and push everyone away. This view of the world can cause you

to isolate yourself from friends, family and romantic partners. This self-imposed isolation reinforces the message that you aren't worthy of love and friendship that the bullies tried to instill in you.

The cycle begins anew

The second reaction is to double down and make the commitment to do even more to help people in the future. In your mind, this can seem noble. You are out to save the world single handedly. However, this option sets you up for a bigger failure in the future. You have to face yourself and your insatiable need for validation from others. The sooner you face it, the better.

The one thing that both reactions have in common is that they are extreme. They lack balance. A balanced approach would be for you to take an honest inventory of your time and personal commitments, allowing you to budget your time. You can set aside time for yourself, your career and family responsibilities and see how much time is available to be there for others. You have to learn the hardest word in the English language for a people pleaser: "no."

I still struggle with this one. I'm learning to prioritize which projects are most valuable to me, my friends and family. I commit to the highest priority projects and say no to requests that would stretch me too thin.

It may take years for you to overcome your need for external validation. But it will never happen if you don't deal with the underlying issues. You have to deal with the bullying and the low self-esteem that resulted from that abuse. You will also have to deal with your anger towards those who abused you and the anger that you turned inward on yourself.

Chapter 6
The Punisher

The first three personas or coping mechanisms discussed so far (underachieving, overachieving, and people pleasing) were directly tied to low self-esteem. The punisher, however, is directly related to the anger from the bullying. It shouldn't be a big surprise that you likely have deep-seated anger towards the individuals who bullied you. The problem is that the anger can fester inside and be projected at anyone who gets in your way or ends up in a minor altercation with you. Unresolved anger combined with the trauma from the bullying can lead to bitterness and an overall negative attitude towards others.

The anger towards the bullies is part of the reason for this persona. However, it's not the only reason. You, like many victims of childhood trauma, often accept partial responsibility for the abuse. No matter how much you consciously fight it, part of you likely internalized the message of worthlessness that the bullies forced on you. Part of you believed that there was something wrong with you that caused the bullies to single you out. You might even be angry with yourself because you weren't able to find a way to stop the abuse.

This anger is often quite different for boys and girls because of the nature of the abuse. Male bullies are often more physical with the abuse. So male victims will more likely be angry with themselves for not being physically strong enough or a good enough fighter to stop the abuse. Male bullies also use verbal taunts but physical intimidation is the primary tool used to keep the male victim feeling too weak and inferior to stop the abuse.

Girls may use physical force to intimidate, but are much more likely to use words and social isolation. Female bullies make their victim feel they weren't quick witted enough or smart enough to fight in the war of words. Female bullies are very good at observing their victims and identifying where the victim feels inadequate or self-conscious. The bully will cruelly use these perceived inadequacies as ammunition. They taunt the victim for the very things that make her feel less valuable than her peers. For example, if a girl is overweight, the bullies will choose to taunt the victim about her weight.

This is incredibly damaging to the victim's self-esteem. The victim now feels that if she were pretty enough, popular enough, or smart enough the bully wouldn't have had anything to target. The female victim will feel angry at her perceived inadequacies and turn that anger inward where it eats away from the inside.

Pushing the anger deep inside

During the bullying, you had no power or ability to fight back. If you attempted to fight back, the abuse increased in retaliation. The bully or bullies had enough physical strength or social clout to deliver more physical and/or verbal abuse for your daring to stand up to them. You quickly learned to push the anger down and not fight back. Looking at the bullies with anger or disgust could be seen as a slight and brought about more abuse. You learned to not only keep your mouth shut but to lower your eyes and physically cower.

Pushing the anger deep inside does not eliminate it. On the contrary, it multiplies. The anger grows as you nurse it. Every time the bullies abused you, more anger was added to the bubbling cauldron deep inside. Anger and shame may have pushed out all positive thoughts and emotions. The anger ate away at you from the inside and may now distort your view of the world.

The anger didn't magically go away

After you left where the bullying was occurring, you might have believed that everything was ok. You left it all behind. However, if the anger has not been dealt with, it doesn't go away. It is still there, buried deep. It can bubble up anytime you are in even a minor conflict. Your reaction to the conflict is far more severe than the situation calls for. It will shock the person who is the target of the aggression and anger. It may shock you and make you wonder where such anger came from.

Memories of the bullying will often replay in your mind. Ruminating over the abuse and the pain it caused feeds the anger. This can poison your mind. You may become bitter and angry at everyone around you. You might even have fantasies about hurting or killing the people who bullied you.

Recent conflicts may also be reflected on, and the anger from your past intensifies the conflict. The conflict might have been minor, but you reinterpret the scale and severity of the events in your mind. These conflicts are added to the pain and anger you carry from the bullying.

If you continue to allow thoughts from the past to fuel your anger, it can destroy you emotionally. It may show up

physically in the form of high blood pressure, chest pain, anxiety attacks and other stress related illnesses. You can be hundreds or thousands of miles from the people who bullied and abused you but you still carry the anger around with you. The anger isn't hurting the people perpetrated the abuse, but it can destroy you.

My early life was a perfect example of this. As a young man, I was full of anger and bitterness. Shortly after leaving high school, my body finally decided it was time to become an adult. I am 5'8", but I was only about 110 pounds when I left high school. Within the first two years of college, I gained 45 pounds. I was working out and had gained a lot of muscle. For a while, I became obsessed with getting bigger in the gym. I wanted to get big enough to look intimidating so nobody would ever bully me again.

I walked around like rabid dog looking to strike out at anyone who got too close. If anyone looked at me in a way that I didn't like they would become the target for the anger I felt inside. I got into people's faces and pushed them around. I wouldn't physically hurt women, but I would intimidate them with words and body language. Men, on the other hand, would get the full brunt of my anger. I would fight at the drop of a hat.

Halloween night, 1986, when I broke two knuckles hitting a brick wall, I was attending classes at SIU. I lived nearly three hours away from where I went to high school. The people who bullied me were far enough away that they had no idea I was still angry and bitter from the abuse. My anger and bitterness wasn't affecting their lives but it was destroying me.

Like many punishers, I lost a lot of friends over my anger. People were initially drawn to me but after a short time something would set me off. I would explode and have to ask for forgiveness. Many people would forgive the first incident,

but after seeing my anger directed towards them or others a few times they would end the friendship.

My anger did not allow anyone to get close. I did not make the decision on a conscious level, but on a deeper level I decided that I would never let anyone hurt me like that again. I hurt them before they hurt me. I looked for any reason to push people away.

You might have had similar experiences, pushing others away with your anger. Every time your anger from the bullying damages a friendship or romantic relationship, the hurt that ensues is transformed into anger and added to the reservoir of rage buried inside. Instead of learning from the experience, you subconsciously use the incident as fuel for your rage. You blame your anger on the people who bullied you and become more angry and bitter. This is another downward spiral that can cost you a great deal in you relationships and career.

You may be able to suppress the anger enough to survive in the workplace. However, there may always be a torrent of anger pushing to get out. You might have to fight the urge to blow up at people over minor conflicts. The workplace is often full of small conflicts that have the potential to become major issues. Your anger is always just under the surface, ready to overflow during any of these conflicts. This anger can cause you to over-react and result in you quitting or being fired from multiple jobs.

Becoming what you hate most

The worst part about this form of coping is that you can become what you hate most: a bully. You don't want to give anyone a chance to bully you again, so you push first. Pushing others around will often get you the desired result in the short term. You can quickly pick up on this and pushing oth-

ers around with your words and/or body language may become your standard mode of operation. You can be too close to the behavior to see what you are doing. If you do see it or allow someone to point it out to you, it can be devastating. The realization that you have become what you most despise is a difficult pill to swallow. If you are not ready to face it, you can deny it and become angry at the person who dared to accuse you of something so vile.

I can tell you from experience that it is possible to let go of the anger and the negative effects it has on your life. You can have an attitude that assumes the best in people and isn't easily offended. It is not an easy process. However, you need to realize that the anger was built over months or years of bullying and it won't go away overnight.

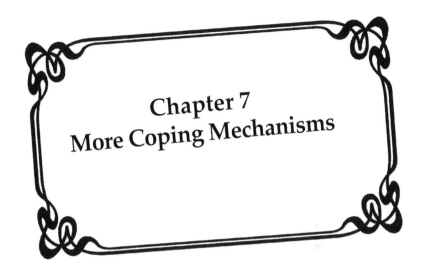

Chapter 7
More Coping Mechanisms

The first few personas came from the low self-esteem and anger over the bullying. They encompassed multiple behaviors and personality traits. You likely identified with some or all of the traits from each of these personas.

Now, let's look at a few very specific behaviors you may use or have used, or currently use, to cope with the pain and anger you carry. Like all negative coping mechanisms, they don't fix the problem or bring any healing; these coping mechanisms only mask the symptoms. They may make you feel better for a short period of time but these prevent you from dealing with the real issues. The true purpose of these behaviors is to make prevent you from feeling the anger and pain. Feeling numb may seem preferable to the pain. However, these coping strategies not only keep you from dealing with the real issues, they have a lot of negative effects as well.

The negative coping mechanisms presented in this chapter (over eating, sexual addiction, drugs and/or alcohol and escapism) are not comprehensive. There are a myriad techniques that you and other victims have used to avoid the pain and go on with your lives. These are only a few of the more common examples of how people cope with being bullied.

If you see yourself in the sections on sexual addiction, drugs and/or alcohol addiction, please seek trusted friends, family or a therapist. These coping mechanisms are incredibly destructive. They can cause you and those around you great physical and emotional harm, quickly destroy every relationship in your life and can even kill you. You will likely need professional help and a strong support network to overcome these addictions. Once you are able to deal with these addictions, you can be in a better position to deal with the underlying issues caused by the trauma from the bullying.

Overeating

The first negative coping mechanism is overeating. This behavior is one of the easiest to fall into because it is directly linked to a physical need. There are three aspects of this coping mechanism that make it seductive. It can relate to pleasant childhood memories, bring about rises in dopamine levels and make you feel like you are less likely to be bullied in the future.

The first thing that makes this coping mechanism seductive is that it can connect with positive memories from your childhood. If going to school meant abuse, Mom's home cooking might have represented safety and comfort. It's more than just taste that can trigger these memories. Have you ever walked into a room where one of your favorite foods was cooking and had the smell of the food bring back memories or associations from the past? Eating is something that can be immersive, involving the senses of smell, touch and taste. The process of cooking and eating can be very comforting and pleasing.

The second seductive thing about this coping mechanism is that it can provide more than psychological comfort. It can also provide short-term physical benefits. These include flavor and chemical responses in the brain. This is especially true of sweets and simple carbs. Sucan can be "...eight times more addictive than cocaine "(Hyman, 2004). Eating sweets activates the dopamine centers in the brain, causing a mild high or type of euphoria. However, after these feel-good chemicals wear off you may experience a low as strong if not stronger that the high you experienced earlier.

This drop in dopamine levels will cause you to crave more sweets or carbs to get the high back. The cycle of lows and highs can wreak havoc on your dopamine receptors. The negative consequences of consuming large quantities of sweets or carbs can lead to weight gain, high blood pressure, and Type-2 Diabetes.

The seductive thing about over-eating is much less obvious but no less motivating. If you were a boy who was physically much smaller than the other boys in your class, you may have become the target of the bullies because you were physically too small to fight back. On a subconscious level you may equate being physically small with being bullied. A part of you believes that if you get big enough, nobody will mess with you anymore. You eat large quantities of food to become big enough to be physically intimidating (Vámosi, 2012). Becoming obese may make you physically more intimidating, but it can cause you to be the target of more bullying as an adult. Many people will shun you or possibly call you derogatory names because you don't fit the ideal body type that is revered in America. Your subconscious attempt to avoid more bullying backfires and actually increases the amount of bullying.

Sexual addiction

Sexual addiction is another coping mechanism that can

be very easy to fall into. Sex, like eating, is normally part of a healthy adult life. However, it can be used in an unhealthy manner. If you are a woman who was a victim of bullying, you likely left school with low self-esteem and a tremendous desire for love and acceptance. Sex can appear to provide both of these and as a woman it is generally pretty easy to find men interested in sex.

If you use sex to get into a relationship, your underlying issues from the bullying may cause problems in the long-term. One possible outcome of using sex as a way to enter relationships is that you are likely to end up with a series of short-term relationships. This has a lot of dangers. One of the most obvious is the possibility of contracting a sexually transmitted disease.

Another danger of using sex to get love and affection is that it can take an emotional toll. A series of relationships also come with a series of break-ups. Each break up reinforces the idea that you are unlovable and that no man will ever love you enough to commit to a long-term relationship. You may try even harder and sleep with more men in an attempt to snag a good catch. This often leads to choosing men who are only after sex, and another negative cycle ensues.

If you are a man who is attempting to use sexual pleasure to avoid dealing with your pain and anger, you may have a more difficult time getting female partners on a regular basis. However, with the advent of the internet, it has become much easier to seek and find plenty of willing partners. If you are married, there are lots of sites that facilitate cheating with lit-tle or no emotional connections.

The dangers for men are not that much different than for women. There is the chance of contracting an STD and the chance of feeling rejected. Men, however, are also in danger of attempting to use sex as a way of feeling masculine. Taken to the extreme, you may go beyond being masculine and become abusive with female partners.

You might go beyond the boundaries of normal sexual behavior. In a healthy relationship, experimentation can be very positive. The willingness to try new things and push boundaries can draw you and your partner closer and allow you get to know each other on a deeper level. However, this is not the case if you are using sex obsessively to avoid dealing with the issues from the past abuse.

In an attempt to fill the need for love and acceptance, you might be inclined to venture into the world of BDSM (Bondage, Domination, Sadism and Masochism). Again, there is nothing wrong with this type of sexual behavior within a healthy sexual life or relationship, but if done for the wrong reasons it can reinforce a negative self-image.

You might play the part of the dominant sexual partner using the dominance to give you a sense of power and authority. You felt like your life was completely out of control when the bullying was occurring, but when in the dominant sexual role you have complete control over another person.

You can also take the opposite role of the submissive. This role can corroborate the way you possibly feel inside. Submission is often more than being under another person's control. As a submissive, you might be spanked, called derogatory names or made to do things that are considered degrading. This reinforces the negative view of yourself that the bullies tried to instill in you and possibly resulted in your low self-esteem.

Alcohol or drug abuse

Another coping technique that you can too easily fall into is abusing alcohol or drugs. These can be legal prescription drugs or illegal drugs. Whether you are using drugs or alcohol, the desired outcome is the same. You are attempting to

become numb to the pain. The altered state obtained through alcohol or drugs allows you to temporarily avoid dealing with your issues. For a while, you can forget about the bullying, the pain, the anger and the deep emotional scars that haunt you.

The effect, however, is only temporary. Once the drugs or alcohol have worn off, the pain comes crashing in on you. In fact, the pain will often be multiplied by the guilt over having succumbed to the drugs or alcohol. You will also have to deal with any negative behaviors that you exhibited while under the influence of the mind altering substances.

If you did anything that you consider shameful or hurtful to others while under the influence, it pushes you to use these substances again to bury the additional pain and shame. This downward spiral is particularly damaging. It can cost you your family, friends, jobs and even take your life.

Escapism

The last negative coping mechanism that I would like to discuss is escapism. Normally, having an active imagination is considered a positive thing. Dreamers are often the people who discover new solutions to problems and create revolutionary products that benefit mankind.

There can be, however, a darker side to having an active imagination when you were a victim of bullying. During the abuse, you were faced with physical and/or emotional pain that was beyond your ability to deal with on a conscious level. One way of protecting yourself was to mentally escape.

You, like many victims, may have created alternate realities in your imagination. These worlds served as escapes from a reality that was too horrible to contemplate. These dream worlds can be very detailed and elaborate. In this dream world, you may have successfully defended yourself against

the bullies and physically, socially or verbally punished them for the abuse they inflicted upon you. In your world, you always fought and won against the bullies. You were the most popular person in the school and earned the affection of the prettiest girls or most handsome guys. When the abuse was at its worst, instead of being mentally in the moment, you could escape to you dream world.

The problem occurs when you use the dream world to avoid dealing with reality all the time. This is especially true if you continue to use this imaginary world after you have left the place where the bullying occurred. This imaginary world can be pervasive enough that it interferes with your ability to deal with your day to day responsibilities.

For example, suppose there is a minor confrontation with a co-worker. Rather than spending mental effort attempting to analyze the reason for the conflict and finding a resolution, you might use your imaginary world to envision yourself winning the argument and humiliating your co-worker. In this scenario, everyone is seen as a potential enemy. In this world there are no compromises. There must always be a winner and a loser. It prevents you from seeking more amiable outcomes and give and take relationships with those around you. There are only adversarial relationships.

This view of the world can keep you from growing as a person. You become stuck in the past, using an imaginary world to cope with the real world. In your mind, you likely still see every person around you as a potential bully or enemy. You are the hero or heroine surrounded by enemies. This view creates a negative thought pattern that clouds how you see the world around you. The adversarial view of others may damage or destroy every relationship in your personal and work life. It can cause you to lose jobs and be the cause of many broken friendships and romantic relationships. If you do not learn to either eliminate this imaginary world, or at

least control the effect it has on your life, it can destroy everything positive around you.

It takes courage to face any of these negative coping mechanisms and deal with them in a mature manner. But it is worth the effort. If, however, you don't deal with the underlying low self-esteem and anger from the bullying, you will be in danger of either going back to your previous negative coping mechanism or falling into a new one.

Section 3
Roadmap to the
Life You Desire

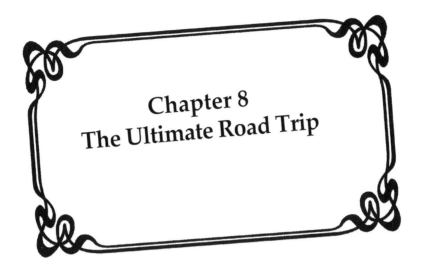

Chapter 8
The Ultimate Road Trip

Did you see parts of yourself in the negative coping mechanisms? Are you still struggling to overcome the trauma and psychological damage from the bullying you experienced? Are you ready to put the trauma and the pain behind you and only see it as a distant speck in the rear view mirror?

It is time to stop traveling down the wrong road with baggage weighing you down. You are about to change direction, and get on the road to a happier more successful you. This road trip will be full of fun, laughter, rest stops, and great places to visit. However, there will be detours, flat tires, and roadblocks. I can't guarantee you the road will always be smooth and the journey easy. But I can assure you it will have more smiles than tears, and will be worth it.

Your road trip will be broken up into four parts:
1. Unloading the car and out of balance tires
2. Balancing the tires
3. Reprogramming your GPS
4. Roadblocks and rest stops

The first three parts of the roadmap involve planning and preparation. The last part is a series of roadblocks that you might encounter and how to navigate through or around them, and a string of rest stops where you can rest and re-charge your batteries before getting back on the road.

It is essential that you first empty the car (yourself) of the baggage from the bad stretch of road you have been traveling on. You can't fit the good stuff in the car you will need for your new journey if it is still full of the old baggage. This will require work on your part, and it will take time. But having the weight of the old baggage gone and seeing the car empty and ready for this exciting new journey will be well worth the effort.

Next, you will need to get rid of the old tires and get new, well-balanced tires that will make the trip much smoother. You will also need to reprogram your GPS to be sure it is giv-ing you the proper directions.

Once you have unpacked the car, balanced the tires and reprogrammed you GPS, you will need to decide on your des-tination. You might find it useful to think about some of the places you want to stop on the way. Your destination will be unique to you. Nobody else can travel the same exact route that you take. It is impossible to visit every great stop along the way, so you will need to decide what stops you most want to visit, and eliminate others. A little flexibility will be need-ed. As you experience new things and learn about new places to visit, you might want to revise your planned route. You might discover a new direction that is better than your origi-nal route and leads to a much different ultimate destination.

As you begin traveling towards your destination, you will encounter roadblocks. You may be able to take a quick de-tour and easily get around them. However, some of these roadblocks may force you to stop your forward momentum for what will feel like a very long time. Hang in there. You

will be able to find ways to get around the obstruction and get moving again.

There will be times that you will feel tired and need a break. The rest stops will be there to give you some down time and help you along your way. There will be tools and tips to keep your car running smoothly and fix minor problems yourself. Each rest stop will specialize in a particular type of service designed to not only give you time to relax and recharge, but make your journey more enjoyable. These stops will be available at multiple points along your journey, so you can find what you need to make your journey fun and help you reach your ultimate destination.

So, are you ready to get started preparing for your ultimate road trip? The next chapter will help you start getting rid of the baggage that has been weighing your car down and taking up too much space.

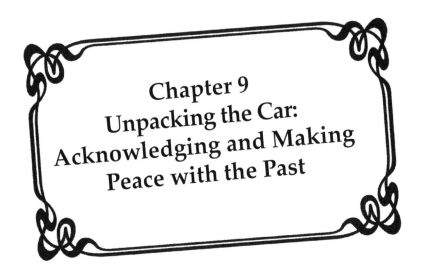

Chapter 9
Unpacking the Car:
Acknowledging and Making
Peace with the Past

One of the biggest issues you might face as an adult who was bullied during your school years is a lack of closure. After you left high school, you were expected to leave the trauma from the bullying behind. The expectation was that you would enter college or a career as if nothing ever happened. There was pressure from society, and possibly your friends and family to move on with your life. Closure is difficult when you don't get the opportunity to deal with the trauma from the bullying.

As a former victim of bullying, you understand that it isn't that easy to just get over it. The verbal and/or physical abuse took a toll. In an effort to move on, you might have tried to conceal the pain, anger, anxiety and other issues you were struggling with. Some of the personas, particularly the overachiever and people pleaser are like mask that make it appear that you've moved beyond the pain. On the outside, you can look like you are successful and/or helping a lot of people. You might have buried yourself in a lot of activates in an attempt to convince yourself that you moved on.

However, when you are alone with your thoughts you

might struggle with painful memories from the bullying. If you don't struggle with specific memories, you might feel like something just isn't right. This uneasy feeling can be in the form of mild depression or a general feeling of malaise or melancholy. You feel down for no identifiable reason. It is possible to have success in your career and/or relationships, yet still feel like something in your life isn't right. It can even make you feel like you are a fraud because your outside success doesn't match up with how you really feel inside. This can increase the feelings of depression or make you feel like a failure no matter how much success you achieve.

If you jumped right into college or a career, you might not have taken the time to deal with the pain, anger and low self-esteem from the bullying. You might struggle with anxiety in certain situations and periodic bouts of depression that seem to come out of nowhere. Just because you chose to move on doesn't mean that the pain you experienced disappeared.

If reading about the long-term effects of bullying has struck a chord, you likely have begun to realize you need to deal with the trauma from the bullying. That realization is a great starting point on the road to healing. Self-awareness is the first step in coming to grips with the pain you carry and the beginning to deal with it.

As you begin the journey of healing, there are a few steps that can help you stay on track. These include making a decision to face your past, evaluating which issues you still struggle with, being patient with yourself and using techniques designed to aid you on your journey.

The first step in getting rid of the baggage from the past is to make a decision to not run from it anymore. You may have been avoiding the pain with lots of activity, self-medicating with drugs or alcohol or finding another way to avoid the pain. You can make a commitment to deal with the bullying and the trauma you experienced.

This can be very scary. It is natural to want to avoid pain, but you have to face the pain from the past to heal and move beyond it. Allowing those painful memories to surface and dealing with them are often important steps in the healing process. The next time you are alone and the memories from the bullying begin to enter your mind, don't reject them or busy your mind in an attempt to avoid the pain. Allow them to surface, but take a step back from the emotions. See the memories as a part of your history and be willing to accept the fact that these memories are traumatic enough that they might be affecting your life now.

Next, you need to evaluate what issues from the bullying you are struggling now. Some of the most common issues are anger towards the bullies, anger towards yourself, anxiety, depression and low self-esteem. Take an honest look at your life now. Which of these do you struggle with, and how often? It could be social anxiety that affects you on a nearly daily basis or short term bouts of depression that only affect you every few weeks or months. Anger and an aggressive attitude might have become your natural way of dealing with people, or it might be anger that only surfaces occasionally during conflicts. Writing down your thoughts can be a great way to truly get a handle on what issues you deal with and how frequently they affect your life.

The next step in making peace with your past is to be patient with yourself and understand that you are human. You went through trauma that damaged your psyche. It is ok to struggle with these issues. The fact that you still struggle with issues from your past doesn't make you a bad person. One exercise that can be particularly helpful is to mentally go back to the time when the bullying was occurring. Take a step back and see yourself as the child or young adult who was going through the bullying. Ask yourself what your reaction would be if you saw another young person going through

what you did. Would you feel angry towards the bullies who were torturing this child or young adult, would you feel empathy towards the victim, or would you want to comfort him or her? Now as an adult, give that younger version of yourself a good dose of compassion and empathy. Realize that the trauma affected you and make a commitment to begin the healing process.

The healing process is not something that will happen overnight, but every day that you embark on this journey it will get better. The last step in the process of healing and making peace with your past is to learn techniques designed to deal with these issues. The rest of this book will help you with implementing these techniques as you begin this road trip. For example, the chapter on forgiveness will be particularly useful if you are struggling with unresolved anger towards the bullies or yourself. The chapters on new tires and reprogramming your GPS will be helpful with anxiety and low self-esteem. Several of the rest stops will also provide simple techniques that will beneficial when struggling with bouts of depression.

Chapter 10
Deep Cleaning:
Forgiveness

After reading my story and the personas and negative coping mechanisms, the title of this chapter may cause discomfort. The bullying occurred during the years when you were developing your self-image apart from your parents and immediate family. Your self-image was impacted more by how your peers responded to you than any other influence in your life. The rejection and abuse from those peers could have resulted in severe damage to your self-esteem and deep seated anger that may have damaged your career friendships and romantic relationships.

Given the damage that the bullying has done, how can I ask you to forgive the bullies who hurt you and intentionally tried to make you feel inferior to everyone else? If this question came to mind, it's only natural. You likely did nothing to bring on the abuse other than exist or be different than what was considered cool or popular. In middle school and high school, being different was enough to make you stand out and become a target for the bullies. You might not have tried to be different; in fact, you probably tried desperately to fit in. You were bullied and abused for simply being yourself.

The reason you need to consider forgiving the bullies is that you need to get rid of the anger and bitterness. You deserve to be free from the baggage that is keeping you from beginning your exciting new road trip. Unresolved anger and an inability to forgive will fill your mind with so much negativity that there isn't room for anything else. The anger and bitterness are like a single dandelion in a yard. If not pulled, the one multiplies till it fills the entire yard. How can you fill your mind with the good things you need for your new road trip if your mind is completely filled with anger and bitterness?

You need to forgive the people who hurt you because you may never experience true freedom and healing until you do. Anger and bitterness over the bulling is a prison that keeps you trapped in the past. You can't live in the present or realistically plan for the future because you are emotionally trapped in the past.

There is an old saying by an unknown author: "Not forgiving someone is like drinking poison and expecting the other person to die". Your anger isn't hurting the ones who perpetrated the abuse, but it might very well be destroying your life. If this anger and resentment isn't dealt with, it can undermine your efforts to heal from the bullying.

You need to come to the realization and belief that forgiveness is for you, not the bullies. You must face the fact that the anger may be hurting you and damaging your relationships. It is likely that you can look into your past and see a string of broken friendships, work relationships and romantic relationships. The bullying programmed you to focus on the negatives and what the other person did to damage the relationship. The bullying was not your fault, and you likely adopted a victim mindset. Part of the victim mindset is blaming others.

If you take an objective view of these failed relationships,

you will see that you often played a part in the failure of the relationships. In many cases, you may have been more at fault than the other person. It may have been a direct result of your unresolved anger, or indirectly from the walls you built to keep others from hurting you. These same psychological walls that keep you from getting hurt also keep others from truly connecting to you. Other factors from the bullying that could be causing issues in relationships include intolerance for certain behaviors, being overly sensitive to criticism or unhealthy methods of dealing with conflict.

There is a danger that as you accept your responsibility for part of the failed relationships, it can further damage your already low self-esteem. It is important that you understand that many of the unhealthy coping skills and a lot of the unresolved anger that you carried for too long were the result of circumstances beyond your control. What was done to you by the bullies when you were young and vulnerable was not your fault. You developed coping mechanisms and adopted mindsets in an attempt to survive the bullying. A few of these might have been positive, but it is likely you adopted some ways of coping that have brought you more harm than good.

Forgiveness is such an important issue that this chapter is divided into two sections. The first section concerns forgiving the bullies, and outlines the forgiveness process. The second section is about forgiving yourself. You need to forgive yourself for not being able to find a way to stop the bullying, and possibly for part of the negative consequences you have brought into your life as a result of the anger and low self-esteem that you have carried with you for years.

It is possible to accept responsibility for your actions as an adult without beating yourself up over those mistakes. If you can see that the anger and resentment from the bullying is damaging your relationships and career, it is time to deal with it.

Defining forgiveness

Before I get into the steps to forgiveness, I want to deal with what forgiveness is not. Forgiveness is not condoning or justifying the bullying or the bullies. Forgiveness also does not mean that you forget what was done. The memories will always be there, and likely a sense of loss over the positive memories from childhood that the bullying robbed you of.

Forgiveness is not diminishing nor disregarding your pain or pretending what happened wasn't painful. It was painful, and these memories may always be painful. However, the pain can be lessened to the point that it no longer causes issues in your life.

Lastly, forgiveness does not mean that you have to reconcile your relationship with the bullies. If you approach the ones who abused you, the bullies may deny it or at least attempt to lessen the severity of the abuse. If, however, one of the bullies approaches you and asks for forgiveness, reconciliation can occur and is healthy. I've had several bullies approach me more than ten years after graduating high school with great sincerity and humility and ask for forgiveness. I have told them I had already forgiven them, but I appreciated their willingness to admit that what was done to me was wrong. I further told them that I wished them no harm, and hoped that they could put the past behind them.

You need to deal with the painful feelings you are experiencing now, not necessarily what you experienced during the bullying. Forgiveness is a process where you are released from the pain and anger from the bullying that is always boiling under the surface. It allowed you to focus on your life now and experience life free from the past. You are getting rid of the baggage from the wrong road you have been traveling on, and creating space for the positive things that will make your new journey more successful and enjoyable.

There are three final points I want to make before I get into the steps in forgiveness. Forgiveness takes effort, it can be painful and it might take time. First, forgiveness will require effort on your part. You may have carried the anger and bitterness for years or possibly decades. It feels normal. The forgiveness process might feel awkward at first. This process also has several steps. Some steps may seem easy, but others will require more effort.

Second, this process can be painful. It means that you will have to deal not only with the bullying, but the trauma and damage to your self-image that the bullying caused. It is natural to want to avoid pain. In this case, however, allowing yourself to feel the pain is a necessary part of the process.

Third, forgiveness is a process that takes time. The bullying might have only been short term or you might have endured the abuse for years. You have now had years or possibly decades of dealing with the painful memories from the past. Time doesn't heal all wounds, in fact many psychological wounds can get worse over time if you replay the trauma.

It took months from the time I decided to forgive until the anger had truly subsided and I felt freedom from the bitterness that was eating me up inside. It was as if there were multiple layers of anger buried deep inside. As I uncovered one layer and dealt with it, another would surface.

Long after I started this process, something would come up that brought back memories from the past and I would feel anger rise up. I would then have deal with the new layer of anger. Each time I went through the process of forgiving, it became easier and more natural. Now I am more easily able to forgive not only past hurts, but even minor hurts from friends and loved ones in the present. I can also tell you from experience that the freedom you will experience is worth the effort.

The forgiveness process

There are several steps involved in the process. They are acknowledging the hurt, allowing yourself to experience the pain, making a conscious decision to forgive, separating the bullies from the abuse they inflicted on you and releasing the anger and the bullies.

The first step is to acknowledge the hurt. You have to consciously acknowledge that what was done to you was wrong. This may seem overly obvious, but many victims hide from this realization. You may go as far as describing your childhood to others as happy and healthy. Before you can heal from the trauma, you have to face the fact that the bullies used their physical and/or social power to abuse you. It was wrong and painful. Not only did the bullies cause you emotional and/or physical pain, they robbed you of many of the positive memories that should have been part of your middle school or high school years.

At this point, it is you might want to get another person involved. Find a friend, family member or counselor who you can trust. It needs to be someone who will not judge you for the anger that you might exhibit and will listen more than give advice. Some people find solace in their belief in God or a higher power. In my case, I feel that God helped me to forgive those who bullied me.

This is where having a professional therapist might be quite useful. A licensed counselor is constrained by HIPPA laws to keep what is said in their office confidential, as long as there is no threat of violence towards yourself or someone else. A counselor's training will be particularly valuable in avoiding the trap of continually reliving the events and reinforcing the trauma. They can help you maintain a more global and healthy perspective, stay focused on the core issues and keep you from going off on tangents that allow you to avoid the pain you need to deal with.

Take time to express what was done to you and how it made you feel to your trusted friend or counselor. A great technique is to write a journal or story that describes what happened to you. The more specific you can be in your description of the events, the better. Part of the problem is separating what actually happened from your interpretation of what happened. People have a tendency to remember their internal story or interpretation of the event, rather than what truly happened. The act of writing the events down makes separating these narratives much easier. Writing can also help you get in touch with the feelings that you may have suppressed for years.

The second step of forgiveness is often the hardest. You have to allow yourself to feel anger and hurt for the abuse on a conscious level. You might have spent years attemping to keep these feelings buried deep inside. These feelings are real and have to be dealt with. I am not recommending that you keep reliving the pain and memories over and over again. That can lead to intensifying the problem. You need to stop burying the pain and allow it to come to the surface. If you began keeping a journal in the first step, reading the journal entries you worked on in the previous step is a good way to get in touch with the feelings you have buried. As you begin this process, allow yourself to feel the pain. You might find yourself crying or screaming at the top of your lungs.

If you have tried to deny or bury your pain from the past, it can be frightening to go back in your memory and allow yourself to feel this pain. As you acknowledge the pain, you will to a certain extent relive it. You may feel it as if it was happening anew. As frightening as this is, it is an important step in getting past the pain. You have to allow yourself to grieve from the pain and the loss of what could have been.

The next step of forgiveness is to make a conscious deci-

sion to forgive. Remember, forgiveness does not excuse what the bullies did. At this stage you are acknowledging that not forgiving will keep you from being free and that forgiving those that hurt you will bring freedom from your hurt and anger. This may sound like a simple step, but to genuinely desire to forgive is a tough thing to wrestle with. Holding onto the anger might have become comfortable. You may want to be free from the anger but it has been a part of you for a long time. You have reached the point that you truly want to forgive those who hurt your without holding onto any animosity.

The desire to forgive needs to be more than a surface decision. You have to mean it in the deepest part of your consciousness. You have to want the freedom from the anger and bitterness so much that you are willing to let the bullies off the hook for what they did. That is not as easy as it may sound. Every time you think about the bullies, pain and anger may immediately come to the surface. If you commit to the process, you can think about the bullies and the abuse they inflicted without a lot of emotion being attached to them. It takes time, but it is possible.

The next step is to separate the abuse from the bullies. What they did was wrong but they are human. This is not excusing their behavior, but rather acknowledging the bullies' humanity. Those who abused you have the same weaknesses and frailties that you have. They might have been abused when they were young or been bullying out of a need for acceptance. The reason that the bullies hurt you is not as important as realizing that they are flawed beings.

The leader of a group of bullies is often the one who controls the rest of them. The other bullies participate out of fear that if they don't go along with the bullying they will become the targets themselves. They don't want to participate, but the fear of becoming a target is stronger than their person-

al objections. This doesn't excuse what they did, but again points to their humanity. These bullies were in a way victims themselves. Many of these bully-victims have feelings of self-loathing from the memories of the abuse they inflicted on you and other targets chosen by the group's leader.

The last step of forgiveness may prove to be especially challenging. You must release the anger and the offenders. This is a decision to release your right to revenge and the anger that you have been holding onto. You make a decision to no longer desire to get even with the bullies for what they did and to release the anger that is buried so deep inside. In this step you release them from your need for revenge and make a decision to release yourself from the pain. In fact, it you might want to make a decision to desire that the bullies find peace and healing in their lives.

In this step, visualization is very useful tool. Create a mental picture of yourself free from pain and an image of the bullies free from your anger. I often pictured myself walking out of a jail cell, unlocking the door and letting the bullies out of cells as well. Imagine feelings of joy as you release yourself from the pain. The more you can get your emotions involved in this more positive response to the bullying, the better. If you began keeping a journal back in step one of this process, it may be helpful to burn the journal entries where you wrote what was done to you and how you felt about the abuse. As you burn the paper, allow the pain and anger towards the bullies to symbolically burn with the paper.

Be patient with yourself

This last part of forgiveness might take time. Making a decision to release the pain and desire for revenge is only a start. You need to begin monitoring your feelings and reactions to events. When memories of the bullying or thoughts

about the bullies cause anger to rise, acknowledge it and make a conscious decision to release it. Every time you go through this step, you will likely feel a weight lift off of you. The first time you do this it is very difficult and may feel fake, but it gets easier with each instance. You might have to fake it till you make it.

As you go through the forgiveness process, you may feel immediate relief. However, your feelings might not change right away. As you commit to the forgiveness process, and start taking the steps listed, the negative feelings will begin to fade. It may take months to see true transformation, but if you stick with the process it will happen.

Forgiving yourself

The last part of this chapter may be the most difficult part for some people. You must not only forgive those who hurt you; you must also forgive yourself. You, like most victims of bullying or other abuse, probably took part of the responsibility for the abuse on yourself.

The steps to forgiving yourself are very similar to ones you utilized in forgiving the bullies. One of the most difficult steps here is admitting that you feel like part of the bullying was your fault. Many victims don't want to face this and wrestle with this concept for a while before they can admit it to themselves. You likely know that there was nothing you could have done to stop the bullying, but on a deeper emotional level a part of you might still struggle with this concept.

You may also have internalized the messages from the bullies that you are worthless, or that you did something to deserve the abuse. When you are told that you are less valuable than your peers over and over again, it is only natural to start believing it. Here again, you know on a conscious level that you are as valuable as anyone else but that seed of doubt was implanted deep in your psyche.

Once you have admitted that you partially blame yourself, you can look inside and begin to see how it has hurt you. You might have sabotaged many positive relationships in your life because deep down you didn't feel like you deserved good things. You must not only admit that you partially blame yourself for the bullying; you must admit that you have sub-consciously used this blame to punish yourself. You might have hurt others with your anger and pushed people away who cared for you or tried to help you.

You can allow yourself to grieve the lost opportunities that the anger and pain have cost you. This is not easy. You can likely look back at your life, and it is like looking at the aftermath of a tornado. Jobs, friendships and romantic relationships lie scattered and broken behind you. It can be devastating to realize how many relationships and career opportunities you've lost in the years since you left the bullies behind.

As you look back at how much the pain and anger has cost you, you may struggle with a lot of negative emotions. It is important that you keep a sense of balance. You can't go back and change the past, but you can begin to make positive changes that will make your future brighter.

Releasing the anger you feel towards yourself is difficult, but hopefully you have already gone through this process and forgiven the bullies. If so, you have become skilled at releasing the anger and need for revenge and you now need to practice this skill in your own life.

Acknowledge the hurt that the pain and anger from the bullying has brought into your life. Allow yourself to experience the pain that the anger and self-loathing have caused and make a conscious decision to forgive yourself. It should be a little easier to separate your humanity from your actions, yet may be more difficult to release the anger and yourself.

Similar to forgiving the bullies, forgiving yourself will take time. It will likely be a process you will need to repeat many times.

Forgiving the bullies and yourself will bring not only release from a lot of pain and anger, it will also free up a great deal of mental energy. You will be able concentrate more of your energy towards your career and personal relationships.

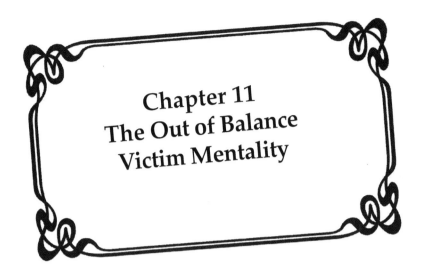

Chapter 11
The Out of Balance Victim Mentality

Making peace with your past and going through the forgiveness process should have already resulted in your feeling lighter. You have emptied your car of part of the baggage that was taking up a lot of space. Now it is time to balance the tires so you can stay on track on your new journey. Your attitudes and overall outlook on life are your tires. They determine which direction the car is pulling you towards.

The victim mentality causes your tires (attitudes and outlook) to be out of balance. It is hard to keep the car going in the direction you want, because the steering wheel is always pulling in the wrong direction. If you take your eyes off of the road or relax your grip on the steering wheel for even a few seconds, you can run off the road or into oncoming traffic. By the time you arrive at a destination, you may feel like you have been fighting the car to stay on the road. It can be exhausting.

There is a simple way to determine how balanced your outlook is. Take time to listen to your internal dialogue and the tone of that voice. You, like everyone else, has an internal dialogue that is constantly running through your mind. It is a nearly constant stream of thoughts expressed through words and images. You might never have paid attention to the tone of these thoughts and images, but they have a huge impact in your life.

The tone of this inner dialogue is one of the biggest factors in determining how successful you are in your career and how healthy your relationships are. If the pervasive thought pattern is negative, your words, attitude and body language will likely be negative. You will attract negative people to you, and push more positive people away. Your thoughts are out of balance and always pulling towards a negative pattern of thoughts and actions.

As a former victim of bullying, your internal dialogue and outlook on life have likely been programmed by the trauma to be negative. For example, if you are passed up for a promotion, the negative thoughts will begin crashing in on you. You may mentally play back your failures at work or what co-workers had done to sabotage you over and over again. These thoughts are added to your self-loathing or anger and can cause you to fall into depression. Your language at the job may become increasingly negative until you lose the motivation to do the work. Your body language and work ethic can suffer, causing you to be at risk of losing your job.

Unfortunately, this negative thought pattern is often normal for you and other adults who were bullied. You were a victim and without a change in your thinking you may always feel that way. Everything that happens to you is filtered through this perspective.

The victim mentality is completely out of balance. It effects many areas of your life. This mentality can affect how you view trials, cause you to always blame yourself or others, and influence your tolerance for risk. Additionally, it can distort your view of the future, affect how you handle humor, keep you trapped in the past, attract more negative people and events in your life and cause you to sabotage your own success.

The victim mentality views all trials as permanent. For example, if you are laid off from your job, you believe you will never find another job. You'll replay the events that led up to being laid off or fired over and over again. The company may have laid you off because it is downsizing but you will see it as either something you did wrong or that a supervisor wants to get rid of you.

When you are trapped in the victim mindset, you are likely to feel that everything that happens requires a person to blame. In the case of being laid off, you will either blame yourself or someone else instead of realizing it is simply a part of business.

Romantic relationships

The effect on your romantic relationships can be even more damaging. If there is a break up, you will likely either blame the other person or yourself for the break up. But there will always be someone to blame. It can't possibly be communication problems or a lack of compatibility. One person has to be at fault. If you blame the other person, it reinforces your view of yourself as a victim. You may enter the next relationship with a more damaged view of what a romantic relationship should be.

If you blame yourself for the breakup, you are likely to fall into depression. The voices of the bullies telling you are worthless and that nobody could ever love you will echo in your mind. Your already damaged self-esteem is in danger of dropping even lower. There is a danger that you could turn to food, alcohol or drugs in a futile attempt to become numb and stop the video of your failure from playing over and over again.

In an effort to avoid the pain and negative emotions, you may enter another relationship prematurely. It could be a co-dependent relationship, or the other person might be attempting to be your knight in shining armor and rescue you. The chances of getting into a healthy relationship when you jump into it too quickly are pretty slim. The chances of a healthy relationship become less likely when avoiding pain or loneliness are the primary motivations for entering that relationship.

The future

As a victim you will likely see the future as hopeless because you expect that nobody will ever give you a chance to succeed. Other people will always keep you down and you are powerless to change it. This is especially true in your career. There is often a tremendous amount of unfulfilled potential when you have a victim mentality.

Every failure is added to the ever growing list of events in which you believe you have been unfairly treated. Each time you fail it reinforces your view of the world. You may get to the point that you believe everyone is out to get you or hurt you in some way.

If you have a victim mentality you may struggle with humor, especially if it involves teasing or hassling in a fun way. You will often take good natured teasing seriously. You can hide the fact that you are hurt, but you become hypersensitive to any criticism. You might also become angry over something that was completely done in a spirit of fun.

Not only will you see the future as bleak, but the victim lives in the past. You replay all the negative things that were done to you again and again in your mind like a looping video. Every time something negative happens, you blame yourself or the other person and add that event to the video. Because

of this, you tend to over-react to every negative stimulus. If someone gives you constructive criticism, you connect that with the real abuse inflicted on you by the bullies and any real or imagined abuse done to you by others. The people around you often feel like they are walking on egg shells and can't be honest with you. Of course, this causes the end of a lot of friendships and romantic relationships, which you blame on others. Each lost relationship is added onto the mountain of abuse that you have built in your mind.

Who you gravitate towards

The worst part of this type of thinking is that you are likely to attract more abuse and victimization. If your thoughts are negative they will show in your words and body language. You will have a scowl or frown. The body language you exhibit will speak louder than your words. The negativity you exude will likely attract people around you who also think negatively. Your friends will spend most of their time complaining about the negative things in their lives and the people they believe are holding them down.

Conversely, if your thoughts are positive overall, this will show. You will have a smile or at least less of a frown. Your shoulders will be held straighter and your overall demeanor will be positive. Making eye contact with people will be easier, you will smile more and your body language will be more open and invite others to talk to you. As a result of your positive attitude and body language, you will attract more positive people around you.

Not only do your thoughts determine what type of people you will gravitate towards, these thoughts will determine your tolerance for risk. When a new opportunity presents itself, it often has risk. For example, you might be offered a job or promotion that includes more responsibility and pay. If you have a victim mentality, you will spend most of your time thinking about the responsibilities, the longer hours and the cost of failure. You may even talk yourself out of the job due to your fear of failing.

The victim mindset can furthermore cause you to self-sabotage when opportunities present themselves. For example, if you get a promotion you may assume that you won't be able to handle the responsibility. That fear can become a self-fulfilling prophecy. You might not take action when needed or use the authority that comes with the position in the way you need to. Your fear prevents you from doing what is needed to succeed.

This same self-fulfilling prophecy can occur in romantic relationships. If you get any attention from an attractive person, your victim mindset can cause you to assume the person has ulterior motives. After all, why would someone who has lots of choices be interested in you? Your fear of rejection and failure can keep you from taking the risk and attempting to start a romantic relationship.

The victim mentality, and the pessimism that comes along with it, can cost you many opportunities, friendships and romantic relationships. You may often fail by default in your career and personal life, because your aversion to risk keeps you from seizing the opportunities presented to you. The downward spiral of blame and anger that results, whether directed at yourself or others, can be toxic.

The negative thought patterns can fill your mind to the point that there isn't room for any positive thoughts. You can't focus on beginning the new journey, because your thinking is out of balance. You keep getting pulled towards bad stretches of road.

So, let's take a look at what more balanced tires look like. A more balanced perspective will allow you to focus on reaching your destination and spend less energy fighting to keep the car on the road.

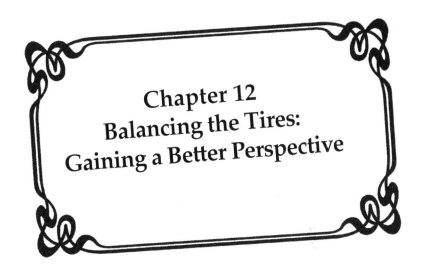

Chapter 12
Balancing the Tires: Gaining a Better Perspective

It will be much easier to follow the road to your new destination if your tires are balanced. The victim mentality represented out of balance tires. You can replace the tires, but if they are the same type you had before, the results will be the same. The tires you have now, your attitudes and outlook, need to be more balanced. To restore a sense of balance, you have to change the way you see the world.

You have to understand what a more balanced view is before you can begin to take action to change it. A good way to start the balancing process is to understand how the victor mentality differs from the victim mentality and begin working towards changing your outlook. One of the biggest differences is how victors view trials. Victors see trials as temporary. If they get laid off, they have confidence in their ability to find another job. If a romantic relationship ends, they know that there are lots of other fish in the sea. They know that they have enough good qualities that other potential partners will be genuinely interested in them.

People with a victor mentality are not unrealistic in their optimism. For example, a recent college graduate will not expect to immediately get a job as the CEO of a major corporation. The victor understands that they will have to start near the bottom of the ladder and work their way up. Their outlook, however, is vastly different from the victim mentality. Victors believe that with hard work and dedication, they can move up in any organization. They understand that they might have to get additional training or learn new skills but they have confidence in their ability to climb the ladder. They might not make it to the top, but they know they can advance as their skills and experience increase.

It might appear as if the victor sees good things as permanent. However, that isn't exactly realistic or balanced. A victor understands that all things, including good things, are temporary. Even our life is temporary. This might seem like going back to a more pessimistic mode of thinking, but it isn't negative; it's balanced.

The realization that good things are temporary is not a reason to lament but rather a reason to celebrate. Since people with a victor mentality know that everything is temporary, they can live more in the moment. If they are going through a painful time, they know that there will be an end to the pain. If things are going well, they can enjoy it to the fullest and truly appreciate every joyful moment.

Dealing with failures

One of the biggest differences in these two mentalities comes with how each person handles failures. The person with the victim mentality takes failure very personally, and it affirms their world view. Victors, however, look at failures realistically. They identify their mistakes and factor in circumstances beyond their control. If they made mistakes, they take note of those mistakes and learn from them. They view failure as a temporary setback on the road to larger success.

Failures are seen as opportunities to learn and grow.

There are famous examples of this. Abraham Lincoln ran for the state legislature and lost. He also failed in business, but he knew he could succeed. He went on to become one of our greatest presidents. Thomas Edison failed thousands of times in his attempt to create a viable incandescent light bulb. He was asked how he could be so persistent in looking for a filament that would make the electric light bulb viable after failing thousands of times. Edison has often been quoted as saying "I have not failed 10,000 times. I have successfully found 10,000 ways that will not work." That statement is incredible. He "succeeded" in finding 10,000 ways that didn't work.

A law school student, Carol, taught me a great deal about how your attitude towards simple mistakes can either validate you as a person or damage your self-esteem. One morning as she was walking into the library, I noticed she seemed a little concerned. She told me that she had locked her keys in her car. She said, "For a smart person, sometimes I do stupid things." The statement struck me as different from how I hear most people talk, so I asked her why she stated it that way. She told me that if she told herself and others that she was stupid for leaving the keys in her car that she would be telling herself that she was stupid. Every time she repeated that thought in her head, or worse, stated it to others, she would be reinforcing the message that she was stupid.

She explained that her way of thinking and explaining her mistakes and failures affirmed the way she wanted to see herself and how she wanted others to see her. She told me that everyone makes mistakes like locking their keys in the car. By stating that "for a smart person, I sometimes do stupid things", she was telling herself and others that she was a smart person, but allowed herself to be human and make mistakes.

Even failures that seem to be much larger than simply locking your keys in the car can be valuable. I've often learned much more from my failures than I have from my successes. When I fall short, it is a reason for me to take a step back and evaluate what happened. Sometimes the failure is a result of an action I've taken and I can change it in the future. At other times, the reason for the failure is beyond my control. That is a cue to go in a different direction.

For example, when I first finished my master's degree I wanted to go into project management for multimedia projects. Web and multimedia projects were all the rage when I entered the Interactive Multimedia Master's program in 1999. Students were walking out the door making 50k – 70k working for various dotcom start-ups. The online world was exploding and the opportunities were everywhere. However, less than a year before I graduated the dotcom bubble burst and venture capital funding for start-ups dried up. Thousands of talented young people had studied graphic design, web design, programming, interface design and web architecture. There were a lot of people with the right education and experience but not enough jobs.

I initially failed to find a job in my chosen field, but I didn't take it personally. It was outside of my control. I had specialized in graphic design for the web and I knew I would find a job that was related to my degree. However, it also opened my eyes to something that I would never have expected.

One of my first jobs after graduating with my master's degree was as the campus photographer for Winston-Salem State University (WSSU). I had worked as a photographer before and I knew working in the marketing office of the university would give me the chance to do at least a little graphic design. It wasn't what I wanted to do long-term but it was a step closer to what I wanted. In addition, I met Rudy. Rudy was a public relations specialist with years of experience in

public relations and marketing. He mentored me and taught me many of the skills I use now.

Two months after I started at WSSU, the chair of the Fine Arts department was in the marketing department talking about an ad campaign. At the end of the meeting, he stopped me and asked me to confirm that I had a master's degree. He told me that they wanted to start offering a Digital Photography class to the Fine Arts students. He asked me if I would be willing to create a curriculum and teach the class. I could use the extra cash and I thought it would look good on my resume. So I agreed to work on the curriculum.

I will never forget that first day in class. Prior to that day, I had never given any real thought to teaching. I liked working with children for short periods of time but I had no interest in teaching kids full-time. But this was teaching adults in college. I did a short lecture and moved into the lab portion of the class. We started working on Photoshop basics and the students started getting excited about what they could do with a camera and a computer. By the end of that first class, the students were looking forward to the rest of the course and I felt like I had finally found a place where I belonged. I loved teaching and seeing the students get engaged in the material. I have since taught classes in Business Communications, Media and Culture, Web Design, and Art History. I have also combined my love of tennis and teaching and taught tennis to many people ranging from five to fifty.

Now I have a job that has a variety of web design, graphic design, writing, and project management. The variety keeps my interest and I still teach as an adjunct instructor on the side. No two days are the same and I have to switch gears on a dime. There is a lot of creativity in this job, and the variety fits with my ADHD.

I have done enough project management to know that I would have been miserable if I had obtained a full-time

project management job right out of graduate school. Project management is very high pressure and has little room for creativity. It is strictly management. Not only is it high pressure, it often requires long hours that could take a big toll on my family life. Failing to find a job in my field forced me to step back and change directions. That detour led me to something that I love: teaching.

The ability to look at successes and failures from a more balance perspective helps people with the victor mentality to build a better future. Victors see the future as bright and full of possibilities. They understand that they have the power to shape the future. Victors don't know exactly what the future holds, but they know that with hard work and the right attitude they can achieve a great deal. Thoughts about the future are not filled with dread, but rather a sense of hope and excitement. The dreams of victors are aimed at the sky, yet tempered by reality.

People with a victor mentality also see the past through a different lens than those with a victim mentality. The victors see the past as something that has helped shape them into the people they are today. Therefore, even the painful parts of their past have value. For example, people who were bullied will likely have more compassion for those who are hurting.

Seeing the humor in life

Victors can take a mental step back from circumstances to see the humor in life. The ability to see the funny side of situations is a huge benefit, and can help people who have been bullied to go through trials without being consumed by them. Laughter lifts you above your circumstances and allows you see the bigger picture.

My friend, Rashaun, is a perfect example of this. His wife had a lot of issues during her first pregnancy. She was in and out of the hospital throughout the pregnancy. Rashaun often came to work tired but seemed to be able to smile through it all. He laughed about being a husband, having to deal with the stress and the funny things that always seemed to happen at the hospital. He often laughed about the struggles that they were having in their marriage and how differently men and women handle the stress. His sense of humor was what kept him going through the tough times. Now Rashaun and his wife have a beautiful baby girl and he beams with pride as a new dad. Their marriage is stronger from going through the trials together. If it wasn't for his ability to laugh during the tough times, the difficult pregnancy could have taken a much bigger toll on their marriage.

You can begin to make the change from the victim mentality to the victor mentality and having a more balanced outlook. It takes time, but it is possible.

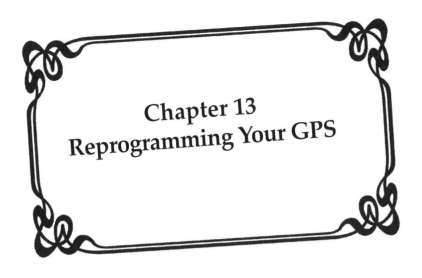

Chapter 13
Reprogramming Your GPS

Your car's GPS will take you on the shortest or fastest route to the destination you plug into it. The manufacturer programmed it to analyze maps and apply an algorithm to come up with the optimal route. This algorithm determines which route is chosen based on a set of criteria. The pre-programmed criteria, your current location, available maps and your destination are all factored in. But what if those criteria or the algorithms are flawed? Have you ever had a GPS lead you to the wrong destination, choose a route that took longer than it should have or chosen roads you didn't want to travel on?

You, like most people, probably believe that you are reacting to events as they happen. However, this is not the case. You react to current situations based on the event itself combined with your experiences from the past. You subconsciously compare this situation to similar situations you have faced before, and decide how to react. It only takes your brain a fraction of a second to comb through your past experiences, find a reasonably close incident and decide on a course of action. Even the way you look at a situation is affected by your past experiences and the way you view the world.

Sounds a lot like how a GPS determines which route you should take to get to your destination. Not only do your past experiences have an effect on your current behaviors, but those memories can change over time. This is especially true of traumatic events, such as the bullying you experienced.

What you remember, the story you tell yourself and others, is different from reality. Your mind replays these traumatic memories over and over again, with minor changes each time. The memory turns into a narrative that gets more distorted with every retelling. These stories surrounding the events in your life become part of a larger narrative that you use to describe yourself.

Replaying the traumatic experiences from the bullying, and often altering them in a way that may make them seem more traumatic, reinforces the victim mindset. That mindset becomes a filter that you funnel every thought and external stimuli through. You take current situations, run them through that filter and decide on a course of action.

Distored filter

You often run current situations through the filter and react to them so automatically that you don't realize you are doing it. Have you ever left your home with one destination in mind, but found yourself turning the wrong way heading for work or school? Your mind can't possibly focus on every stimulus and it is difficult to truly focus on more than one thing at a time. When your mind wanders, your subconscious takes over and puts some task and reactions on auto pilot.

Have you ever found yourself in a conflict with another person and either overreacted with anger or shut down emotionally and withdrew in such an extreme way that you later found yourself asking where that reaction came from? A part of your mind took the current situation, ran it through the victim mindset filter and responded without much conscious thought. The interesting thing is that the more emotionally charged that situation, the more likely you are to have an automatic response. You become conditioned to respond to situations based on how similar they are to past experiences.

For example, pretend you are walking through a thick jungle. You hear leaves rustle behind you on the trail. As you look back, you see a tiger coming out of the bushes. Your body goes into fight or flight mode and you start running. You run and manage to get away from the tiger. Your breathing is fast and shallow and your heart is racing as you finally slow down and catch your breath.

A few days later, you are walking in another wooded area and you hear a rustling in the leaves. Your body instantly reacts. Your pulse quickens and your muscles prepare to run as you glance back. This time, however, it is only a squirrel. You manage to not run away, but your breathing is still fast and shallow and your pulse is still pounding in your ears.

You feel silly for nearly running away from a squirrel but you had very little control over your initial reaction. The incident with the tiger had conditioned your mind and body to equate rustling in the leaves with a tiger and possible death. Over time as you repeatedly walk in wooded areas and hear rustling in the leaves that prove to be harmless, your automatic reaction will likely begin to change. Your conscious mind will take the time to look and see what made the noise, and take the appropriate action. But it will take time. You may, however, always have to fight your body's automatic response to flee for your life.

My mother was a good example of this. She was involved in a terrible car accident when I was about sixteen. She was driving my dad's pickup truck when a car ran a stop sign from a side road and plowed into the side of the truck. The

window of the truck was open and as the truck flipped on its side my mom's arm went out the window. The truck then bounced back up on the wheels. When the truck bounced on its side and her arm was out the window, the top of the cab came down on her arm. Her arm was crushed, and most of the bones in her upper arm were splintered. She had multiple surgeries, and the doctors had to rebuild the bone in her arm from a piece of bone in her hip with pins and screws. She spent two months in the hospital and it took more than a year to fully heal.

When she first came out of the hospital, I had to drive her around because she had a large metal apparatus sticking out of her arm holding the bones together. I was a new driver and nervous enough as it was. Every time a car was late coming to a stop from a side road or seemed to be going a little too fast as they approached a stop sign from a side road, my mom would scream. Needless to say, this startled me the first few times and we nearly ended up in a couple of wrecks. After a few years, my mom was able to not react to every car coming from a side road and I was able to not freak out if she mildly panicked. It took months for her to stop overreacting to cars coming from side streets. It has been over thirty years since the accident and she still gets nervous when another driver appears to be coming too fast from a side road.

These two examples may seem overly simplified. After all, human interactions are much more complicated than walking down a wooded path and hearing the leaves rustle. You also don't go into fight or flight mode with every interaction. However, the basic premise holds true. Your past experiences do have a profound effect on how you react to current stimuli.

You may find yourself in a minor confrontation with another person and feel anger bubble up from deep inside. The current conflict triggers emotions of anger and helplessness from the bullying you experienced. Your mind adds the anger from the past to the anger you are experiencing during the conflict. If you aren't careful, you can overreact to the situation and explode.

Anger from the bullying can condition you to assume that every confrontation, no matter how minor or serious, is a fight or flight situation. When your body goes into this mode, it produces adrenaline and prepares for action. The nervous system reduces your ability to think logically, and you go into auto pilot.

So, if your past reactions have such a strong influence on how you react to current situations, how do you change those reactions? How do you reprogram you mind (GPS) and body to react without being affected by the abuse you suffered from the bullies?

Steps to reprogram your GPS

You can begin to change your internal dialogue and thinking, but it takes effort. It also won't happen overnight. It will take time. There are several steps that you may have to go through repeatedly until your thought patterns become more positive and affirming. But over time, as you continue to take these steps, your outlook will change from victim to victor. To change your mindset, you will need to:
- Admit the bullying affects how you react to current stimuli.
- Understand that your memories of the bullying have changed over time.
- Monitor your thoughts.
- Stop the negative dialogue and rumination.
- Replace the negative dialogue with something more positive or affirming.

It might seem like there are a lot of steps to this process

and it can seem a little overwhelming. With a little practice, however, it will become second nature. Remember that this is going to take time, so be patient with yourself as you start this process. Going through these steps will begin to change your subconscious and you will have a new filter and repro-grammed GPS. Your GPS will have a much healthier and positive set of criteria to work with. When you go on auto pilot, the destination chosen will be much more beneficial in your work and personal relationships.

The first step in this process is to admit that the past bul-lying has affected how you react to current stimuli, and that you have developed some unhealthy ways of dealing with people and situations. You had to find a way to survive and cope any way you could. This may seem obvious, but you may have refused to deal with the pain or buried it because it felt too traumatic.

Along with understanding that your past alters how you react, it can be helpful to admit that those memories have been altered over time as you replayed the events over and over again. You might have minimized the severity of the bullying as part of a coping technique, but if you buried the emotions they are still pushing you to react strongly. On the flip side, you might have made the stories more traumatic as you meditated on them. Like telling a story over and over again, the memories of the bullying have either been mini-mized or intensified.

The next step in changing your mindset is to learn to mon-itor your thoughts and reactions. You don't have to constant-ly be thinking about what thoughts are running through your mind; just be aware of your internal dialogue. As you make a decision to be aware of your thoughts, you will begin to notice the tone of those words. You need to stop obsessing over your problems and the trauma you experienced from the bullying. This is a recipe for disaster. According to Sonja Lyubomirsky in *The How of Happiness,*

> The combination of rumination and negative mood is toxic. Research shows that people who ruminate while sad or distraught are likely to feel besieged, powerless, self-critical, pessimistic, and generally negatively biased (2008).

When you notice that your internal dialogue is negative or has a victim-like tone, you need to immediately change that dialogue. There are several ways to do that. Being aware of the negative tone and making the decision to stop that line of thinking might be enough. You will have taken the dialogue from auto-pilot to something you are consciously focusing on. You can then begin to think about something more positive and the dialogue changes.

The more you practice changing your internal dialogue, the easier it will become. However, there are times that it may seem like your mind is fighting you. If you are struggling to stop the negative dialogue, there are other things you can do to stop it. These include saying "Stop", using a wrist band, and physically changing your circumstances.

The first method of changing your internal dialogue is to say out loud, "STOP." You can say it fairly loud if you are alone or quietly if you are in a room with other people. When you speak the word, it will jog you out of your internal dialogue and into the external world around you for at least a split second. It is very hard to be truly focused on something external, and on auto pilot internally at the same time. This by itself won't change the dialogue, but it will stop it long enough for you to take further action.

A second method of stopping the negative emotions is to wear one of the popular rubber wrist bands. You can look like you are supporting a good cause and have it as a tool at the same time. When you are struggling to stop the internal dialogue, snap the rubber band. You don't have to snap it hard.

Snapping it lightly will get you out of your own thoughts, as you have to deal with the physical stimulus from the minor irritation.

Reverend Will Bowen started an international movement with rubber bands. He created purple rubber bands that said *A Complaint Free World* (2007). He challenged the members of his congregation to wear them and attempt to go twenty-one days without complaining. Any time they complained, they were to snap their wrist with the rubber band, and they had to start their count all over again. Most people couldn't make it a few hours at first but after a while they began to make it several days. It took most people who accepted the challenge several months of practice to make it twenty-one days in a row without complaining, but many were able to achieve that goal.

These people were able to change their thought patterns from complaining towards more positive thoughts and attitudes. They are living proof that we can change our internal and external dialogue. In their case, they changed their external dialogue, and it eventually changed their mindset. The members of this congregation now report being happier overall, and have learned to focus on the positive things around them rather than the negative. What started out as a challenge to Brown's congregation went viral, and they have now sent over 10 million bracelets to people in over 200 countries.

Another great way to change your thoughts is to physically change your circumstances. One of the worst things you can do is sit alone thinking about the bullying or other trauma from the past. Watching television or other passive activities can be detrimental to your mental state. The passive nature of these types of activities does not require you to engage your mind on a conscious level and the negative tone to many news shows or other broadcast can add to the negative mood you are struggling with.

You need to give yourself a task that is engaging for your mind to grab onto. You could do something as simple as go for short walk, play with a pet, call a friend and talk about anything except the thoughts that are plaguing you, go play a sport, hang out with friends who have positive attitudes, read a good book or anything that makes you feel better and takes your mind off of the memories and negative thoughts you are struggling with.

The first few times you try to distract yourself, it will feel like you are running from your problems. But this is not what you are doing. You are refusing to allow your mind to obsess over your problems or the trauma from your past. You are changing your focus from very negative thoughts to positive actions. If you do this consistently, it will work. In general, "truly happy people have the capacity to distract and absorb themselves in activities that divert their energies and attention away from dark or anxious ruminations" (Lyubomirsky, 2008).

A word of caution is in order here. No matter how much you work at not ruminating over the past, distracting yourself and refocusing on positive thoughts, it will not always work. There will be times that your mind will replay memories from the past and you will find it difficult to change your thought pattern. This can lead to further destructive thougghts as you deride yourself for not being able to get beyond the past. Don't get down on yourself when you struggle with memories from the bullying. The trauma you experienced was all-consuming when you were experiencing it, and without any counseling or other guidance about how to deal with the memories, rumination became a deep set habit. What you are attempting to do is retrain your mind (reprogram your GPS) to stop one habit, and develop a new healthier habit. This won't happen overnight. According to Yoni Freedhoff, MD,

...changing behaviors and creating new habits takes

an awfully long time. While you may well be able to establish a comfort level with a new behavior in just 21 days, my experiences have taught me that habit formation requires years of consciously reminding yourself of your new choices (2013).

Dr. Freedhoff quit smoking, and stated that "astonishingly to me, even two to three years after quitting, there were still occasional moments or circumstances when I had to consciously fight the urge to light up."

So give yourself a break and expect that there will be times you will struggle with negative thoughts over the traumatic incidents from the bullying. However, it will become easier to change your focus as you practice using these techniques to stop the negative thoughts and cultivate more positive trains of thought. You will also notice that you struggle less often with memories from the past.

As you change your thoughts, you will change your behaviors and the level of success you achieve in your career and personal life. I like the way that Frank Outlaw summarized the connection between our thoughts, actions and future:

Watch your thoughts, they become words;
watch your words, they become actions;
watch your actions, they become habits;
watch your habits, they become character;
watch your character, for it becomes your destiny (1977)

You can change your life by changing what you think about. You will be drawn to the things on which you focus. If you allow yourself to obsess over the pain from your past, you will not be able to focus on the good things around you. You can begin to take control of your internal dialogue, which will result in actions that are more likely to draw positive people to you as work to make the best of both good and bad situations. These little changes in behavior will have a cumulative effect that will help you achieve greater success in your career and develop better relationships with your friends and family.

In many ways, your brain is like a computer. As the old saying goes, garbage in, garbage out. If you spend your time thinking negative thoughts, you will get negative results. If you spend more time thinking positive thoughts, you will get more positive results. Your life will not be perfect. There will always be hard times and negative things that are beyond your control. But if you develop a more positive mindset, you can have more positive outcomes than negative ones.

Replacing negative thoughts

Now that you have stopped the negative thought pattern, you need to immediately replace those negaive throughs. Your mind will not stay still for long. The GPS still needs to know what direction to point towards.

One great thing you can do is to start thinking about anything positive and change your internal dialogue. Make a conscious decision to think about one or more positive things for a few moments. Find the one or two things in your life you are most thankful for and meditate on these things. For example, do you have a spouse who enriches your life, or a pet that brings you a lot of comfort and joy? Take a few moments and think about positive memories associated with that person, animal or thing in your life. In most cases your internal dialogue will change, at least for a short time.

Several more techniques that can be useful include:

- Take a quick inventory of the people and things you are grateful for.
- Think of something positive that happened that day or maybe the day before. Keep it fairly recent.

- Think about a good thing that is going to happen in the near future. For example, you might be going to a movie or other occasion with friends or co-workers.
- Plan a reward for yourself, and keep it in mind. For example, if you made it through a full day without having a lot of negative thoughts or having to suppress rage and anger, reward yourself with something small that will bring positive emotions. I love to surprise my wife by ordering take out for dinner and renting a good movie. It is fairly inexpensive. Plus, I enjoy cuddling on the couch, appreciating the touching and closeness and watching a good movie. Watching TV alone can reinforce negative thoughts but this activity is much more about sharing time with the woman I love.
- Change your physical environment. Don't stay where you are struggling. If sitting alone at home is making it harder to stop the negative thoughts, go where other people are. A walk in the park, trip to the grocery store of any where ohter than where you are right now, and preferably where there are other people around.
- Call or visit a friend or family member who will lift your mood. Don't call someone who will just coddle the negative emotions.
- Laugh. Talk to someone who makes you laugh or watch a comedy show or movie. If you can combine this with going to another location it is even better. Meet a friend for lunch or dinner who makes you laugh.
- Exercise. A short walk or quick trip to the gym will boost your mood and change your mindset
- Spend a small amount of money on an experience rather than a physical object.

Spending money on an experience that can bcome a pos-

itive memory has a much more lasting effect on your overall happiness than buying something. (Achor, 2010).

Learning to change your thoughts is not a once and you're done kind of process. You might change your thoughts to be more positive yet occasionally find yourself back in a negative or victim thought pattern a short time later. You likely have spent years developing a victim mentality and thought processes. It became a way of coping with the despair and self-loathing you felt inside. Ruminating also became a habit. You not only continually replayed the video of the bullying in your mind, you reflected on the little things that went wrong on a daily basis. Every situation was filtered through this negative mindset. This negative bias may have kept you from seeing the positive things in your life or fully enjoying the good times.

In the beginning, as you go through this process it may feel almost phony. It can feel like wearing clothes that don't fit right; it's awkward. But as you begin to make changing your thoughts a habit, it will begin to feel more natural. You will likely find that you have to stop the negative thoughts much less often. You might even catch yourself smiling as you think of something positive without realizing that your thought process is changing.

Benefits of a positive mind set

In life you often get what you expect, which is big benefit of adopting a more positive mindset. You tend to see what you are focused on. A good example of this can be seen when you buy a new car. Have you ever noticed that after you bought a particular model of car, you started seeing them everywhere? That model of car was there, but you didn't notice it. You can't focus on all the stimuli coming at you, so you "tune out" much of the world around you. You tuned into that car model.

Another benefit of adopting a more positive mindset and shedding the victim mindset is that you are more likely to see success on a regular basis. Success really does breed success. As you succeed in one endeavor and keep making better choices, more doors open. Many of these doors will take you a great distance in a short time. Instead of a slow steady climb, you may find yourself on a meteoric rise.

There is one precaution that you need to be aware of. Like anything else in life, a positive attitude and outlook can be taken too far and throw your tires out of balance. Having an overall positive mindset is great, but it isn't practical to feel upbeat and positive 24 hours a day 365 days a year. Life is full of ups and downs. If you have recently experienced the death of a close relative or friend, lost a job, are going through a divorce or experiencing another traumatic incident, you are going to have a lot of pain and negative thoughts. However, if you are in the habit of seeing the bright side of things, the amount and duration of the pain and negative thoughts will be less. You will still struggle at times, and go through the natural and healthy grief cycle when appropriate. But, you will come through those tough times with more optimism, and be back on a positive outlook much quicker than you did when you were in the victim mode.

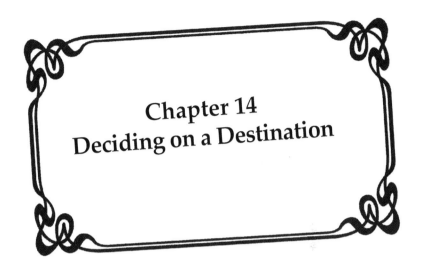

Chapter 14
Deciding on a Destination

As you eliminate negative thought patterns and begin replacing them with more positive thoughts, you may well notice that your natural state is to be more positive. However, for lasting change you need to change where you focus your time and energy. Up to this point, you might have been spending all your mental and emotional energy in an effort to survive, and not planned a route. You might have also set your GPS for a destination that doesn't serve you well or fit with your talents and abilities.

You now need to program a new destination into your GPS. One that fits with your talents, personality, life goals and dreams. One issue is that as you look ahead there are thousands of possible destinations. There are, however, a few steps that you can go through that will help you narrow the choices of destinations and decide on the best route to get from where you are now to where you want to be.

These steps are:
- Getting clues from your past and current motivations and destinations
- Determining your core values

- Defining your priorities
- Using the Unlimited and Deathbed metaphors
- Programming in your new destination

Your past motivations and destinations

A great place to start is to take an inventory of your life as it is right now. What has motivated you to make the life choices that have led to where your current destination and shaped the person you are today?

Don't just look for the negatives here, but all the motivations and decisions. Have you avoided risk because of low self-esteem, or did you have unresolved anger that damaged your career or personal relationships? On the flip side, did you channel the anger in a positive way and use it to work harder and succeed in areas of your personal or business life? Did the pain from the bullying help you be more compassionate towards others who were hurting? Have you managed to climb the ladder of success or are you still struggling in a dead end job?

Your age will also make a difference. Are you fresh out of high school and starting out in college or the workforce? If so, your financial resources are likely more limited but you have a lot more time to get where you want to be. There is a chance you don't know what you want, which is fine. You have plenty of time to figure it out.

If you are older, you probably have a better handle on what you want and don't want out of life. You likely have more financial resources, which can make it easier to change direction. However, you may have more responsibilities that constrain you. It can be more difficult to change direction in your career as you get older. It is possible, but it takes more planning.

In my case, as I began to do an inventory of my life I realized that I had been motivated by a desire for revenge against the bullies, my anger over the bullying and my self-loathing. I blamed myself for not finding a way of stopping the bullying. I saw myself as a coward and a failure.

I also viewed everyone around me as a bully, or at least a potential bully. It was difficult for me to trust anyone. That view of others caused me to say and do things that sabotaged many personal and business relationships. I had to rethink what I wanted in my career and personal relationships.

So, right now, please take out a piece of paper and begin writing down details about where you are now. Include information about your career, where you live, how you spend your free time, who you are in a relationship with, if you have children and their ages and any other pertinent information about your life right now. Once you have completed writing notes about your current condition, begin thinking about the choices you made that brought you to where you are now. Making additional notes about these motivations is quite useful.

Take time to think about the motivations behind the choices you wrote down. How many of those were made from positive motivations, and how many were made from fear or other negative motivations? As you look back at your past choices and motivations, did the trauma you experienced from the bullying affect why you made some of these decisions? If so, write those down and resolve to not allow that trauma to affect your choices in the future.

Being aware of how the trauma affected you will make a huge difference. The next time you find yourself in a situation where you have to make a major decision, you will be more aware of your motivations. As you face major decisions in the future, take the time to think about the motivations behind why you are leaning towards one decision or the other. If the pull of fear, low self-esteem or other negative emotion from the bullying is pulling you in one particular direction, re-evaluate your position. Determine to make decisions based on what you want and where you want to be, not on fear or other negative emotions.

Your core values

Now that you have taken a good look at the decisions and motivations that have contributed to your current situation, you need to begin deciding where you want to go from here. A good place to begin is to look at your core values. What is really most important to you, as you move forward? You need to look beyond the surface to what you place the most value on.

Some examples might include loyalty, integrity, spirituality, fairness, hard work, family, honesty, work/life balance, helping others or creativity. What values do you aspire to exhibit in your own life? How can you begin to incorporate one or more of these in a more effective way in your life? Ask yourself that question on a regular basis, maybe even daily, and start making one small change at a time that will ensure that you are living by your core values. It is hard to feel happy and fulfilled if you are not living in harmony with these core values.

Writing an initial list of these core values down is a very good idea. Just, be aware that as you discover more about yourself, you might find that those core values are not what you originally thought they were. You might find that you have not been living your life in harmony with these core values.

You may discover that you have spent so many years traveling on auto pilot or having the wrong destination that you aren't one hundred percent sure what your core values are or should be. It's ok if you feel a little lost. Think about what

matters most to you and what values you want to aspire to most. Write down your thoughts, and begin to narrow them down to your core values.

Many people I've known have never taken the time to identify their core values and make life changes to align with those values. For example, I know one man who said family was what he valued above all else. However, his singular focus on his career wad causing him to lose his family. He worked long hours and was rarely there for his kids sporting events or recitals. His wife finally left him and he was forced to look at the difference between what he said was important and what he showed in his actions. Thankfully, this friend was able to re-evaluate his life. He took a lower paying job that allowed him to be home more, and he and his wife reconciled. His marriage has survived and he is much happier, although he has less money and doesn't have the big office.

Priorities

Your core values were intangible things like honesty, integrity and spirituality. Your priorities are much more practical. These are about who and what are most important to you on a more tangible level. Think about the people and things in your life that are most important to you. If another person was to look at your life from the outside, how would you want them to see you spending your time, energy and money pursuing? Some examples include family, career, charity, artistic expression, frugality, saving for your kid's education or retirement, taking a yearly family vacation or seeing different parts of the world.

What is truly important to you? Write down a list of what comes to mind. Begin with a general list, and be prepared to change it as you discover that what you thought was most important isn't as high on the list as it should be. These should be things that are not short term, but what you genuinely want to accomplish at this stage of your life. For example, maybe becoming wealthy is one of your highest goals, but after really thinking about it, you want to put family higher on the list. After you make your list, take a look at how you're spending your time and money. Are you living in harmony with these priorities?

Here is a list of my priorities:

- God
- Family
- Friends
- Writing and publishing my book
- Career
- Physical exercise
- My hobbies (tennis, photography, hiking and bowling)
- Wealth

When my days begin getting crowded with too many activities, I go back to my list. Am I living my life according to my priorities, or am I letting other areas of my life take up so much time that they are interfering with my highest priorities? If I find that I'm not living in harmony with my priorities, I make changes that work towards getting the way I spend my time to match up with those priorities. I've changed jobs or refused promotions that I felt would interfere with my relationships with my wife and son. It has meant that I didn't have as much money as I always wanted, but the tradeoff was well worth it.

Looking ahead, how can you begin to make changes today so that how you spend your time and energy lines up with what is most important to you? Do you need to begin looking for a new job or possibly go back to school to get that degree you have always wanted? Do you need to focus more on the relationships with your family or friends?

Are you willing to sacrifice in the other areas to make your life line up with your priorities? For example, if education is one of your biggest goals, you might have always wanted to get your bachelor's degree. If you need to work full-time, are you willing to sacrifice time with family, friends, hobbies and other interest to put in the hours studying? Would the long-term benefits of the degree be worth the short term sacrifices? You might discover that this would be a good time to start or you might decide that getting the degree needs to move down on the priority list for now.

Your core values change slowly because they are based what you are at a very deep level. Priorities are much more flexible and can change as you go through the stages of life. In the education example, you might have decided that right now is not the time to finish the bachelor's degree. It may need to wait till your kids are older or other situations have changed. As your kids become more independent, getting the degree can move higher up on the priories list.

Nobody can tell you what choices to make. Trust your instincts. As you have adopted a more positive mindset you have also reprogrammed your mind (GPS) to be more positive and seek what is best for you. Even when you don't know what to do on a conscious level, one way will often feel right where another direction feels off. Do an internal check to be sure that you aren't acting out of fear or anxiety.

The right decision should not only feel right, it should bring with it a sense of excitement or enthusiasm. Often the direction you need to go will scare you or at least make you feel a little uncomfortable. If you feel a lot of excitement, but have some angst over the cost of failure or the level of commitment it will take to accomplish your goal in pursuit of one priority it might be the best course of action. Many people feel most energized and see their biggest rewards when they are stretching and being pulled out of their comfort zones.

Unlimited metaphor

The concept of thinking about what you want might be new to you if you have spent most of your energy surviving. There are a couple of simple exercises that can help you begin to get a handle on what you really want to do and where you want to go. These exercises are not meant to show you exactly what you need to do with your life. Their purpose is to identify where your interest are and what you truly value. They are only starting points, but can prove useful in discovering who you want to be and what is most important to you.

These exercises are in the form of two metaphors, the unlimited metaphor and the deathbed metaphor. As you go through these exercises take the time to not only think about these scenarios, but write your responses down. Writing your responses down makes it easier to sort through the clutter and focus on what is truly most important.

The first exercise is the unlimited metaphor. Open your mind and allow your emotions to get involved as you imagine that you have unlimited money, talents and resources. What would you do for a career? You might be tempted to say you would retire, but many people who retire early suffer from depression and health issues. Work is a way that you contribute to the world around you. It provides a sense of self-worth and brings a sense of accomplishment.

What would you do if you weren't getting paid for it? For example, I love teaching and speaking so much that if I were independently wealthy I would still teach.

What would your typical day at work look like? Would you work with people or do you prefer to work alone? Would you work with details or the big picture? Would you manage others, have a boss or be an entrepreneur? Would you work in an office or outside? Would you work with your hands creating something, work in front of a computer or work in a gym or other active place? Do you work better in a fast paced environment, or in a more laid back low-pressure environment? The more details you can come up with, the closer you will be to figuring out what you want to do for a living.

What type of person would you want to be in a romantic relationship with? Do you want a person who enjoys staying at home or someone who loves going out and doing things? Do you want a lot of physical affection or do you prefer to have more space? Would you prefer a partner who loves many of the same hobbies and interest that you could do together or would you prefer someone who has very different interest that would allow each of you to have more of your own separate identities?

Who would your friends be and what qualities would you want them to exhibit? Do you prefer to hang out with a small group of people that you have very close relationships with, or do you like to hang out with a large group of extroverts and have interactions with a lot of different people? Do you like to hang out with people who are adventurous and thrill seekers or people who prefer more low key activities? Do you prefer to be around people who are a lot like you and have many of the same interest or with people who are much different than you and pull you out of your comfort zone? None of these are wrong or one better than another. What matters is that you find what appeals the most to you.

What activates would you want to do during your free time? Are you into sports, creative hands-on crafts, photography or other arts, reading, learning, watching movies with friends or just hanging out and talking with friends and family?

What do you dream of accomplishing outside of your main job? For example, writing and publishing this book was one of my bucket list items. Do you want to write your own book, visit certain places, run a marathon, get a college degree

or have other personal goals that would give you a tremendous sense of accomplishment?

Where would you live? Do you prefer the beach, the mountains or a farm in the Midwest? Do you prefer to live in the middle of a busy, bustling city or in a rural area with lots of land and privacy? Would you have a big house with lots of bedrooms and multiple floors or a simpler home that is easier to take care of?

Allow yourself to not only imagine having unlimited money and resources, but try to really get into it. Visualize yourself actually doing these things and get your emotions involved. Feel yourself cuddling on the couch with that special person, hitting the perfect shot on the tennis court or shaking hands as you close the business deal. Feel your hands wrap around the steering wheel as you drive your dream car. Imagine the feeling as you walk into your dream home. The more real you can make the experience in your mind, the more motivated you will be to achieve your dreams.

Deathbed metaphor

The deathbed metaphor is almost a mirror image of the unlimited metaphor. Imagine you are on your deathbed. As you look back at your life, what would you want to say your biggest accomplishments were? What would you want to say you had left the world? What would you want your family and friends to say about you after you are gone? What memories would you hold most dear?

On the flip side, when on your deathbed, what would you regret the most? What would you wish you had accomplished in your personal life, your relationships and your career? Who would you want by your side in your last days or hours?

One thing that often becomes clear on the deathbed metaphor is that the relationship side of the equation has more weight than the career side. If you have ever spent time talking with a person near death, what they did or didn't accomplish in their career is normally not as important as their relationships with their family and friends. This doesn't mean that there is no value in what you accomplish in your career, but it can serve as a reminder to make time for the people in your life while you pursue your dreams.

It helps if you take the time to write your responses to these two scenarios. Those responses will give you something that you can refer to when you feel like you are getting off course. Your answers to these exercises and your priorities might change as you grow and mature. New experiences will change your perspective and major life experiences will alter your priorities. For example, if you are single right now but get married and have kids, your wife and kids will become some of your highest priorities.

Did you discover anything new as you went through these mental exercises? Did you find any big discrepancies between where you want to be and where you are now? A few of the desires you had with the unlimited metaphor were probably unrealistic. After all, you don't have unlimited financial resources or talents. But there were probably general qualities to your ideal work life, relationships and geographic location that are within the realm of possibility.

It might take time to get from where you are to where you want to be, but you can start making small changes every day that will point you in the right direction. These exercises weren't meant to show you exactly where you need to be, but will get you started thinking about what is most important to you and what you want out of life. They also can alert you that you might be pursuing goals in your work and/or personal life that are in direct opposition to what is really most important to you.

Even if you never see some of the things you want in life completed, you will be much happier if you are going in the right direction. People often feel much more fulfilled during the pursuit of a goal than they do after achieving that goal. Have you ever known someone who spent years working to get a degree or to finish a big goal that felt a big letdown after finishing the goal? So, start moving towards your goals. The journey truly is more important than the destination. Dream big but take small steps every day towards your dreams. Each step will bring you a little closer to your dreams, and you will find the journey to be exciting, challenging and rewarding.

Your career

Now let's look at one of the biggest areas of your life, your career. People who work at a full time job usually spend more waking hours at work than they do at home. Since you spend so much time and energy in your job, shouldn't it be something you enjoy and feel energized by? According to a recent poll, 52.3% of Americans are unhappy at work (Adams, 2014). It is sad to think that more than half of the people at work don't like their jobs. They are working for a paycheck and counting down the days till retirement.

If you are a college student, this is a great time focus on what you want to do. A particular degree or job experience doesn't lock you into a job for the rest of your life. One of my former bosses, Laurel, completed her Juris Doctorate (law degree) but discovered she didn't like working as an attorney. What she did love was legal research and writing, which is why she did well in law school. So she got a Master's of Library Science. The two degrees allowed her to get a job as a law librarian at SIU (Southern Illinois University), where she retired from. She not only loved legal research, she loved helping the law students learn how to do the research they needed to complete their degree.

Laurel loved her job, despite the fact that there were parts of it she didn't care for. She was the best boss I have ever worked for. Her enthusiasm for learning and research was contagious. She motivated me as I was working full time and taking classes for my master's degree. When I would get tired of researching and writing, she would remind me that the goal of doing what I love would be worth the effort.

For those of you who are already in the workforce, I understand that you might not have the ability to quit your current position. After all, you have to make a living for yourself and possibly a family. You might have a mortgage, car payments and other expenses that make you feel like you have to keep your current position.

If you discovered something in the unlimited metaphor that led you to believe you are on the wrong career path, it is still possible to begin moving closer to where you want to be. If your experience isn't directly related to what you want to do, you have likely developed soft skills that can make the transition easier. For example, you might have developed the ability to sell your ideas, persuade others, manage budgets and projects or any other skills that are needed in multiple careers. These soft skills can bridge the gap from where you are now to where you want to be.

There are different paths to get from your current position to where you want to be. You can take your passions and talents and begin making changes that move you in the direction you want to go. Here are three possibilities:

- Gaining experience by working part time while keeping your current position
- Volunteering or doing a part time unpaid internship in a desired field while keeping your current position
- Starting a small side business while you keep your current position

Not only will these strategies possibly help you move into a career better suited to your abilities and interests, they give you a chance to try your hand at the new field before jumping in full time. You might find that the field you were looking into is not what you want to do. For example, you might like working with computers and be considering changing to a career in Information Technology. However, as you begin working part-time in IT, you might discover that you don't enjoy the fact that you have to often deal with difficult people who are upset because their computers aren't working properly. You might enjoy it enough that dealing with these people is acceptable, or you might find that it isn't worth it.

There are many people who have used one or more of these strategies to change careers and now love what they do. For example, I have a friend who loves photography. He started taking photos of friends and family for a nominal fee as he gained experience, used the profits to purchase better equipment and worked hard to hone his skills. He then started taking larger projects such as team and individual photos of little league teams, cheerleading squads and other kid's sports. His small business started growing, and when he was making about 75% of his full time income on the side, he quit his full time job. Now he owns his own studio. He often puts in long hours as a business owner, but loves every minute of it. He is earning a much better living than he did before and looks forward to going to work every day. His wife and kids often help out with the business as assistants on shoots taking money, posing subjects, setting up lighting or whatever else needs to be done. He is full of energy and his enthusiasm and love for photography are contagious.

Not only will working a job you don't enjoy feel like a prison sentence, the stress can affect your health. The stress can lead to high blood pressure, heart problems, a reduced ability fight off infections and weight gain. The emotional toll of working in a job you hate can also be quite damaging to your personal life.

There are additional downfalls to continuing to work in a job you don't like that are less obvious. One very detrimental effect is the bad example you are setting for your children. If you hate your job, your children will view work as a negative thing. Do you want your children to see an example of someone who drags themselves to a job they hate every day, or a person who loves what they do and sees their job as a way to fulfill their potential and contribute to the world?

If you don't begin to follow your passion in your career, you are robbing others of the gifts and talents that you could be using to improve their lives. Going back to the example of my friend who now owns his own photography studio, he has a real gift for revealing the true essence of his subjects in his portraiture. His clients are often amazed at how his portraits not only make them look their best, but capture who they really are. If he wouldn't have followed his passion, he wouldn't be enriching the lives of his clients.

As you examined your core values, established your priorities and went through the unlimited and deathbed metaphor exercises, you should have gained at least a little more of an idea of where you want to be in your career and relationships. It is unlikely that you will have pinpointed exactly where you want to be, but you should have a general direction to set your GPS towards. You can probably point to a great place you would like to visit that is in the general direction you want to go. For example, you might not know exactly what you want to do for a career, but know that you like to figure out how things work. That sounds like the work an engineer does. You can begin taking classes part time towards an engineering degree, and see how you like them. As you take classes, you may discover one particular type of engineering, appeals to you more than others.

Don't be afraid to set your GPS in a particular direction, even if you are not 100 percent certain it is where you want to go. You can always change directions if needed. Nothing is set in stone. Experiences that don't turn out to be what you want to do long term still have value. Any career or personal skill that you acquire is a good thing. If nothing else, the experience will help you learn more about what you don't want. Sometimes knowing what you don't want can be nearly as valuable as knowing what you think you want.

It is far worse to remain stagnant in a place where you are miserable than to step out and possibly have to change directions again. Even if you end up going off on a tangent, at least you are moving forward. Being in a job you hate or in a relationship that makes you feel miserable is like being stuck in a pit full of deep mud in a cold pouring rain. It is miserable staying where you are but difficult to move forward with the mud pulling on your feet. It can be so difficult to move forward that you resign yourself to being stuck in the cold rain. If, however, you begin moving forward, you will likely find dry land and shelter are much closer than you realized.

You might think you are too old to make a major change in direction. It may be more challenging to change direction as you get older, but it is possible. There are great examples of people who have made drastic changes or started new ventures later in life and had great success. Some of these include:

- Colonel Sanders didn't open his first Kentucky Fried Chicken restaurant till he was over 40. He had been a steamboat driver, worked as an insurance salesman, and for a short time, was an attorney. A physical fight with a client convinced him to stop practicing law. He opened a service station and began serving food at the station. That lead to his desire to serve meals that people could take with them on the road, and KFC was born.

- Peter Roget published his Thesaurus at the young age of 73.
- Abraham Lincoln failed in business and had a lackluster political career, including losing the race for senate, until he won the presidency at the age of 51.
- Grandma Moses was 78 years old when she began painting. She started selling paintings for 2 and 3 dollars, but eventually many of her paintings were sold for thousands of dollars. In 2006 one of her works was sold for 1.2 million dollars.

You can begin finding your passions and pursuing them at any age. Start taking the time today to discover your ideal career and personal relationships. Your path will likely not be straight. You will take unplanned detours and have to find your way back on the right road. But if you keep searching, you will find that the more you learn the closer you will be to locating the best destination for you.

The process of discovering what your passions and talents are and how to use them to improve your life and the lives of others requires that you don't stay on auto pilot. You have to be watching the road for signs pointing to exciting new destinations that may come up and be willing to go on unfamiliar roads that make you feel a little uncomfortable. Growth is rarely easy, and can often be painful. But living your life in a way that is in line with your core values, spending your time and money pursuing your highest priorities and becoming the best version of you possible is worth the effort.

As you begin searching for the path that is best for you and are willing to change direction as needed, you will likely find others that are traveling similar paths. Some of these people will help you overcome obstacles and discover new roads you didn't know existed. You will also discover that your outlook on life will become more positive as you get closer to finding the best route to take. You may encounter others

on your journey who have lost their way, and are wandering aimlessly. You can help them find their way back to the right path, and helping others brings a tremendous amount of joy and fulfillment.

Chapter 15
Roadblocks

You should now have at least a general direction to set your GPS towards. You might even have decided on the first stop on your longer journey. As you begin this new road trip, it is important to understand that you will encounter roadblocks. These may be in the form of failures, fear of success, social comparisons, negative life events, and depression. Some of these roadblocks will not only halt your forward momentum; you might find yourself losing ground or going in the wrong direction for a while.

Failure

The first roadblock is failure. No matter how much you endeavor to make the right decisions, you will make mistakes. Some of these mistakes will be very minor, but others will be more damaging. Everyone fails.

There are some examples of this from very well-known people. Michael Jordan went home and cried after not making the varsity basketball squad his sophomore year in high school and later became the greatest players of all time. He once stated, "I've failed over and over and over again in my life and that is why I succeed."

Henry Ford is known for his innovative assembly line and American-made cars. However, he wasn't an instant success. He failed several times in his attempts to start his own business. He even went broke five times before he founded the successful Ford Motor Company.

Many famous and successful people failed before finding their personal road to success. For example, Walt Disney was fired from the Kansas City Star because his editor felt he "lacked imagination and had no good ideas" (Gillett, 2015). Steven Spielberg was rejected by the University of Southern California School of Cinematic Arts multiple times. While developing his vacuum, Sir James Dyson went through 5,126 failed prototypes and his savings over 15 years. One of my favorites is Thomas Edison whose teachers told him he was "too stupid to learn anything."

Failure may be an inevitable part of life, but it doesn't have to be the end of your life. In fact, failures are often where we can learn the lessons needed to become truly successful. Think back on your own life. Has you ever had a failure that taught you a valuable lesson?

When you fail, it is ok to stop your forward momentum and regroup. Allow yourself time to grieve. You are not only grieving the failure, but the loss of what might have been. If you failed at something you put your heart and mind into it is only natural to feel a sense of loss. You don't, however, have to stay in the grieving process so long that you never get started again. As the sting of the failure fades with time, go back and look at the situation. Despite the failed at the attempt, you probably did some things right. Take an inventory of what worked and what didn't. Avoid making the same mistakes in the future, but don't be afraid to try something new.

For example, I learned a lot from the failure of my first

marriage, including a great deal about what not to do when facing marital strife. The experience forced me to go to counseling for a second time and deal with the remaining issues from the bullying that I still struggled with. It also forced me to go back and take another inventory of who I am and what's important to me.

As you look back at your own life, are there failures in your career or personal life that helped you learn valuable lessons that led to bigger successes later on? Did you have a relationship that failed, but revealed more about yourself and made you a better partner for the next relationship? Did you ever lose a job, but found a much better job afterwards?

Fear of success

An unusual roadblock that you might encounter is the fear of success. Why would you fear success? After all, you want to achieve your dreams in your career, your finances and most importantly your relationships. Being a former victim of bullying, however, success is new. If the bullying affected your self-esteem enough that you've failed at nearly everything you've tried, you know how to handle failure. It is familiar. Plus, failure reinforces the low self-esteem that the bullying left you with. This can turn into another vicious cycle. You feel your aren't worthy to have what you really want in life, so you sub-consciously do things to sabotage your efforts. This causes you to fail repeatedly, which reinforces the belief that you aren't worthy of success and leads to more failures.

It can get to the point that you cease striving to succeed. You find a place where you are relatively comfortable and feel safe. You know you aren't fulfilling your potential. A part of you aches to do more, but if you don't step out and give it your best effort you don't have to face another failure. It becomes easier to maintain a state of mediocrity than to step out and take a chance.

Beyond the fear of stepping out of your comfort zone, there are several reasons that as a victim of bullying you might fear success. These include heightened expectations, taking away your ability to complain, fear of the unknown, the possibility of leaving friends and family behind and fear of losing your identity.

The first issue with success is heightened expectations. If you give it your best and you succeed, everyone will likely expect that higher level of performance from you on a regular basis. This can bring with it a lot of pressure to perform. If you have failed enough, the people around you stop expecting much from you. That means you can get by with minimal effort. The longer you have maintained this level of performance, the scarier it will be to step out and attempt to perform at a higher level. As you achieve more success, you have farther to fall if you fail. Conversely, if you never attempt anything new or push to succeed, you don't have far to fall.

The next reason succeeding can seem like a negative is that it takes away from your ability to complain. Even if you don't admit it, part of you likes to complain. When you feel that you have no value and you have failed at most things you try, there's a lot to grumble about. Most of your conversations revolve around the negatives in your life. In fact, if you are in that place you probably have a group of friends that complain to each other about how hard your life is. You and your friends Commiserate about how difficult your life is, but they never challenge you to do better. Plus, if you didn't complain, what would you have to talk about?

If you stop complaining, you might have to find a whole new set of topics to speak about and a whole new outlook on life. The people you currently hang out with might not want to be around you anymore, or you might find that you no lon-

ger enjoy hanging out with that same group of complaining friends. So, not only would you have to stop whining, you would have to possibly cultivate friendships with different people.

There is also the fear of the unknown. If you have one success, it will lead to another door which will lead to yet another opportunity. Before long, you could find yourself in an entirely new place where you don't know the rules. That would force you to stretch far beyond your comfort zone. Fear of the unknown can be crippling when the bullies conditioned you to feel worthless. The unknown means more chances to be hurt or ridiculed. It may feel much safer to find a place where you can hide in the corner and not draw attention to yourself.

Another reason to fear success is that you might leave friends and family behind. Success may mean that you surpass your friends and family. As you grow, they can remain stagnant. This causes you to grow apart. The further you go, the greater the distance between you and those you love. Some of your friends and family will cheer you on, and possibly grow with you. Others, however, might resent your successes or personal growth. They may feel that you are getting "too big for your britches." They may become jealous as they see you going beyond where they are comfortable going. A few of your friends and/or family might attempt to sabotage your attempts to succeed in order to keep you from leaving them behind.

One last reason to possibly fear success is that you might be afraid of getting so caught up in the search for success that you lose who you are. You likely know someone who is an over-achiever; that person who is obsessed with obtaining wealth or their career.

For example, a former boss of mine put in over 70 hours a week for years. He had reached the executive level, but had sacrificed his relationship with his family in the process. His

kids were now grown and he was coming to the realization that he had no relationship with his children beyond money. The only time they came to him was when they wanted money. He never made it to any of his kids' soccer games, or extra-curricular activities. He missed their major milestones and it was too late now. Fortunately, he realized his mistakes and determined not to make the same mistakes with his grandchildren.

You don't have to fear success. The world needs your gifts and talents, and you deserve to see the success that comes from using those gifts and talents to their full extent. It will be scary and you will find yourself feeling alone and afraid at times. That isn't always a bad thing. Thank back to something that scared you and how much of a sense of accomplishment you felt after you conquered your fear and tried it. It could be speaking in front of a group the first time, going back to college later in life, or participating in a new sport or hobby that pushed you out of your comfort zone. You have likely tried something that scared you and found out you enjoyed the experience once you stepped out.

As you begin pursuing your passions and start seeing successes, you might have friends who fall away. However, you will find new friends who will believe in your and see all that you have to offer. They will encourage you. Some of these new friends will have succeeded in areas where you are attempting to succeed and may become mentors.

Social comparison

Another road block that you need to be aware of is social comparison. This is difficult to avoid, especially in the western world. Advertisements in magazines, on television and online constantly bombard us with images of men and women who have a great deal of money, huge homes, fancy

cars, perfect figures, stunning spouses and perfect kids. We are told things like drinking certain sports drinks will make us as good as our favorite athletes, using certain cosmetics will make women look like movie stars, driving the right car will make us look more successful and that wearing the perfect clothes will make us the envy of all around us. One of the biggest ways we get hooked is ads telling us that if we eat certain foods or participate in certain exercise programs that we will have six pack abs and perfect beach bodies.

These ads encourage us to compare ourselves with the people in the advertisements, feel that we fall short and buy whatever they promise will elevate us to the same level as the models. No matter how hard we try, most people will never be able to measure up to the perfection that is put in front of us. Even the models and celebrities can't live up to the expectations placed on them. This is one reason that many celebrities end up in multiple divorces, struggling with drugs and/or alcohol addictions or do other things to self-destruct. The pressure of striving to live the perfect life and be examples, while constantly in front of the cameras is incredible. Their private lives are scrutinized. The tabloids and celebrity gossip shows seem to revel in letting everyone know when celebrities fail, and the public seems to be eager to see them fall.

The media also encourages us to compare ourselves to other people around us. We are told that we must have the prettiest house, nicest lawn and best car in the neighborhood. There are car ads that show one person being jealous over his or her neighbor's new car or seeing how perfectly green and manicured the neighbor's lawn is.

Everything, including what we do for a living becomes a type of contest or a way of sizing each other up. When two people meet, especially men, one of the first things they ask each other is, "What do you do for a living?" Often the person who asked first is itching to brag about the status or income that comes with their job. Normally, one person ends up feeling superior to the other after this question is answered. This sets up a social hierarchy, or pecking order, that is tough to break out of.

Social comparison is a trap that will bring down your level of happiness and often cause the end of friendships. If you are constantly attempting to establish your place on the social ladder, you will find it difficult to truly celebrate the accomplishments of others. You will likely feel torn between wanting to support and be happy for the other person yet feeling jealous that it wasn't you who got the promotion, raise or recognition.

Comparing yourself to others will also make you less happy overall and add to your stress level. According to Sonja Lyubomirsky in her book The How of Happiness,

> ...the happiest people take pleasure in other people's successes and show concern in the face of others failures. A completely different portrait, however, has emerged of a typical unhappy person—namely, as someone who is deflated rather than delighted about his peers (2008).

If you find yourself struggling with this particular roadblock, remember that nobody else has traveled the road that you have. The person you are comparing yourself to didn't have the same beginnings or the same struggles and successes along the way. Anytime you engage in social comparisons you will either feel down because you have less than others or superior because you have more. Neither of these feelings will help you get to your destination because you will be focusing on the road someone else is taking instead of the road ahead. You can become so focused on watching everyone else drive that you run off the road. So, determine today that you will focus on your own journey and spend less time looking at what others do or do not have.

Traumatic life events

As you continue on your ultimate road trip, you will run into several roadblocks in the form of negative or traumatic life events. These incidents may include the death of a loved one, losing a job, divorce or any other occurrence that takes a big emotional toll. Similar to the reaction to failure, you will have to go through the grieving process.

It can be tempting to go back into the victim mindset. Allow yourself to grieve, but don't stay there. Don't allow your genuine pain to pull you back into the victim mindset. Give yourself time, then set your GPS back on course. Some traumatic events are so poignant that they change your perspective. It may be useful to go back through the exercises of identifying your core values and priorities as well as the unlimited and deathbed metaphors.

Hopefully, you will have friends and family to help you through the tough times, but they need to be the kind of friends who will not let you stay down for too long. A good friend will wait till the time is right, and remind you of what you do have. That friend might give you a proverbial kick in the seat of the pants to gently push you back on the road to success. They can also help you maintain a healthy perspective.

Depression

You may or may not be a person who struggles with depression, but the trauma that you suffered from the bullying makes it much more likely that you do. Everyone has bad days, and traumatic life events will bring sadness as part of the grieving process. Depression, however, is more than just a bad day. The difference is the severity and duration of the bad feelings. When the sadness begins to interfere with your

work and enjoyment of recreation, interferes with your sleep and possibly begins to affect your health, you need to find a way to get beyond those feelings.

It's ok to have negative thoughts and to struggle with depression. You don't want to stay there. Long term depression is incredibly destructive and can take the joy out of your life.

Please don't stay in a depressed state for long. Some of the rest stops will prove very helpful in dealing with depression. Choice, physical exercise and gratitude are particularly effective tools to get out of and stay out of depression.

If these rest stops are not enough to pull you out of depression, it might be useful to see a professional counselor. You might have to take medications to get through some bouts of depression. Ask for help and get back on the road to where you want to be.

Chapter 16
Rest Stops

As you begin your new road trip, you will find there are times that you are tired and need to take a break or times that you realize that you've gone off track and need to get back on the right road. Rest stops are techniques that can help you recharge and get back on the road towards where you really want to be, or ways to maintain your vehicle to prevent you from breaking down on the road. These rest stops include choice and visualization, setting goals, having fun, physical exercise, gratitude and service, religious affiliation, meditation/prayer, taking a positive personal inventory and having more flow experiences.

Each of these rest stops will be useful at different times and places along your journey. If you are struggling with negative emotions that are causing you to be pulled off course, you don't have to keep fighting to keep the car on the road. It is normal given the trauma from the bullying that you might occasionally struggle with memories from the past or negative emotions connected to the trauma. These memories of the bullying, negative thoughts and/or depression might be normal, but they don't have to be your reality all the time. The next time you are struggling with issues related to the bullying, try some of these techniques and see if one helps.

The power of choice and visualization

One technique that is particularly helpful is using the power of choice and visualization to redirect yourself and get back on course. If you are struggling with negative emotions, take a minute to go back to the notes you have written down from the unlimited and deathbed exercises. Look at something you want to be or somewhere you want to go. Right now choose to take one step, no matter how small, in the direction of one of your dreams. For example, if one of your goals was to get a college degree you could look online at colleges where you are considering taking classes. Look at the classes you will be taking in their online catalog. If you want to get an additional boost take another small step and fill out the application to one or more of your chosen colleges or send an email to a representative to take a tour of at least one of the campuses.

Similar to what you did with the unlimited metaphor, use your imagination to visualize yourself further down the road towards your goal. Really get your emotions involved. See yourself getting an A in the first class, making friends with other students who are seeking similar degrees or walking across the stage and shaking hands with the college president as you accept your degree. Feel the texture of the leather of the cover as they hand you the degree. Smile as you wave to your friends and family and feel the sense of accomplishment as you walk off the stage with your degree in your hand. The more specific you can make the scenario in your mind, the more your emotions will follow.

Choosing to do anything that moves you closer to where you want to be and using your imagination to envision the end result will change your emotions. Your mind can't tell the difference between something that actually happened and something you vividly imagined. Your emotions respond as if you had actually completed that goal and had the experience.

The cool thing is that you can now use those new positive emotions to spur you on to further action. While you still feel the sense of accomplishment at getting the degree, take another step in that direction. Maybe start reading online materials that might be used in the new degree, or begin looking at jobs that the degree will likely lead to. Find out what a typical day would be like in the job that you are preparing for. You could find someone in your area who does what you want for a living and ask to take them to lunch to interview them about their job. Not only will this get you more excited about getting the degree, it will become a connection that could open doors to get a job after you finish the degree. The idea here is to use another action to reinforce the positive emotions.

It is very hard to stay emotionally down when you are visualizing something you want to accomplish or a place you want to be. There are two keys to making this change in emotions last. You have to choose a goal that is truly obtainable given your talents and abilities and you have to continue to take positive steps towards that dream or goal.

Choosing a goal that is attainable, given your abilities and opportunities, is a big part of making the change last. For example, getting a degree is an attainable goal for most people. You might have to work harder to achieve it than others, but it is possible.

Some goals, however, are unreachable and set you up for failure and negative emotions. If you are middle aged or older, say in your 50's or 60's, you probably won't be able to obtain a spot on a professional football team. No matter how much you exercise and work to improve your skills, it's very unlikely that you can compete with the much younger men who play professional football.

The second thing you need to do to make the change in emotions last is to take that one small step towards your goal. You could sit on the couch visualizing yourself getting the degree and it might change your emotions for a short time. However, it won't have the same impact as it will if you combine that imagined experience with a step towards that dream. Combining these two will give you a true sense that you are not only dreaming of getting that degree, but that you are actually moving ever closer to achieving your dream.

You've likely heard the quote from Chinese philosopher Laoz that "a journey of a thousand miles begins with a single step." It may be a cliché, but it is true. Each tiny step you take puts you closer to your destination. As you begin moving forward, you will know you are headed in the right direction. There is a peace and a sense that your life is getting better when you are heading towards your dreams. It almost feels like you are heading towards home, even when you have never been to this place before. It is where you belong, and in your heart you know it.

If you start feeling like you can't reach your destination, you can look back at how far you've come and it will inspire you to keep going. For example, if you have to work full time and can only take one class a semester towards that degree, it may seem to take a long time to finish it. It might appear as if you will never finish the degree, which can make you feel down or defeated. But if you take a look back, you can see the classes you have taken and the grades you have received. You might not have finished the degree yet, but you are closer than you were. Looking back, you can see what you have accomplished so far and then re-imagine yourself completing the degree and getting the job you want.

Setting goals

You might have a dream that you know you are capable of obtaining, yet it is so far away that the distance seems too long and the journey too difficult. One way you can prevent being discouraged by the distance you have to travel is to break it into a series of shorter road trips that will get you where you want to be. You might have 1000 miles to travel, but you can chop it into shorter trips as well as plan to stop and rest at interesting places along the way.

Have you ever tried to drive a long distance and found yourself getting too tired to go on after driving for several hours? You might have stopped and spent the night somewhere before continuing. Do you remember how refreshed you felt when you got up the next morning and hit the road? After getting a good night's rest you were ready to continuing toward your destination, and ended up enjoying the trip instead of dreading every mile.

You can set your GPS to take you to places where you can get much needed rest and possibly find something to inspire you as you continue on the next leg of your journey. For example, I have a friend who wanted to go into nutrition. She knew she would need to get a bachelor's degree, a master's degree and finally do an internship as part of the process. It would be a six to seven year process. As she finished high school, the journey seemed too long, and the final destination so far away that it was overwhelming. She focused on the smaller destinations she would need to reach along the way. As she entered college, she concentrated on getting her bachelor's degree. She didn't worry about the master's degree until her junior year, when she started applying to graduate schools. By that point she was more than half way

to her bachelor's degree, and looking further ahead towards graduate school didn't seem as frightening or overwhelming. Once she started graduate school, she started looking for internships.

Setting smaller goals allowed her to keep the finish line within sight. Plus, when she finished one section of the journey, she could look back and see how far she had already traveled. This was especially true after she finished the bachelor's degree. The four year degree took as long as graduate school and the internship combined. When she got frustrated taking graduate level classes, she could look up on the wall of her dorm room and see the framed bachelor's degree hanging there. She now works as a nutritionist and loves helping people improve their lives through better eating habits.

Although you need to make your smaller goals attainable, they also need to be challenging. Making your goals too easy can leave you feeling restless and bored. Achieving what you truly desire in life is rarely easy. Choosing to stay where you are and not pursue your dreams will likely leave you with a sense that your life is not all it can be. Every day you choose not to take at least one step towards your dreams is a day lost to mediocrity.

You can decide today to begin pursing your dreams, and that will require setting goals that challenge you and push you out of your comfort zone. As you set your GPS on shorter destinations along the road to your ultimate goal, you will have to get past obstacles on the road. There is a sense of accomplishment that you can look back on when you find yourself discouraged and are tempted to stop pursing your dreams. You can look back and see times when you have overcome tough obstacles in the past. You may see that it was during these past struggles that you experienced the greatest personal growth and maturity.

I see this need for challenge on the tennis court on a

regular basis. Not only do I play tennis, I frequently watch matches between other players. One of the most frustrating things to watch is a match where one player is completely outmatched by his or her opponent. The stronger player gets bored, and the weaker player becomes discouraged. Neither player feels good about the experience.

If, however, the opponents are closely matched in skill and physical conditioning they will push each other to play better. Both players end up feeling like they are playing well, no matter who wins. They both walk away with a sense of accomplishment knowing they gave it their all and performed at their best.

I personally enjoy playing a person who is a little bit better than I am; it pulls my game up towards their level. I might not win, but I often end up playing well enough to give the better player a challenge. There is tremendous satisfaction in pushing yourself beyond your normal limits and seeing that you can do more than you thought you could.

The bigger your ultimate goal or farther away your ultimate destination, the more you will need to break it up into smaller goals that can be obtained in the short term. The sense of accomplishment as you reach the smaller goals and the realization that you are moving ever closer to your ultimate goal will be needed during tough times.

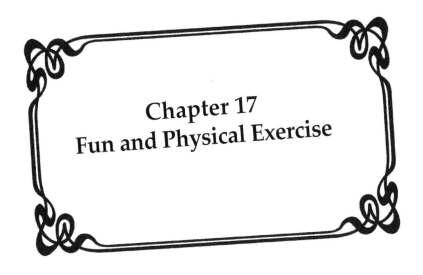

Chapter 17
Fun and Physical Exercise

These two rest stops are great for stopping negative emotions and getting back on course quickly. It may seem overly obvious that going to have fun would be a great way to improve your mood. However, when you are struggling with depression, painful memories from the bullying or negative thoughts, going out to have fun is the last thing you want to do. You likely want to lie in bed and hide from the world, sitting on the couch watching TV and eating junk food, drinking alone or whatever it is that makes you feel comforted and allows you to hide from people. I completely understand. I used to sit and graze on junk food watching movies as a way to hide from the world when I was struggling with memories from the bullying.

Your natural inclination is to avoid people and find something comforting. The problem with this strategy is that it reinforces the negative emotions. You begin taking the wrong road and make it harder and harder to find your way back to where you want to be. Also, the longer you indulge in these comforting activities the deeper you are likely to fall into negativity and/or depression

Not only will these comfort seeking activities push you deeper into negative emotional states, some of them are incredibly destructive. For example, watching TV and eating junk food can lead to obesity, which can create a multitude of problems including high blood pressure, diabetes and joint pain. As you gain weight, it becomes more and more difficult to get off the couch and exercise, which makes it even more tempting to vegetate on the couch and eat to help you feel better.

Drinking too much has obvious health problems and lying in bed is an almost guaranteed way to fall deeper into depression. Each of these comforting activities turns into a cycle of negative consequences that make you feel worse and encourage you to engage in more of the detrimental activity. Another thing that nearly all of these activities have in common is social isolation. As you isolate yourself from others, you create a breeding ground for negative emotions. Spending a great deal of time alone means that you aren't spending time developing friendships. The lack of close friendships makes you feel lonely. The loneliness adds to the depression and makes you want to engage in the negative comfort activities even more. This becomes another cycle where you isolate yourself, making you feel lonely, so you isolate yourself further which leads to more loneliness.

Have you ever found yourself in one of these cycles that seems to pull you deeper and deeper into loneliness and depression? As the negative spiral continued, did you find it harder and harder to climb out of the preverbal hole you were digging yourself into? You don't want to go down these roads.

There will be times that you will feel down, and you legitimately need to take a little time to yourself and do something that feels comforting. It is ok, for example, to sit and watch a movie and eat a small amount of junk food once in a while when you have had a really hard day. Just don't make it a daily habit. You will have times that are legitimately rough, and you will need to do something that brings you some comfort and allows you to recharge your batteries. But there are healthier and more effective ways to deal with negative emotions that will serve you better.

Having fun

A great way to stop the negative spiral is to go out and have fun. There is a bigger benefit to this if you find someone who has a similar interest to do the fun activity together. Maybe you like to go shopping. Buying something new has been shown to have a great short term effect on your mood (Atalay, 2008). However, it is usually short lived. But the time spent building the friendship has a much bigger benefit to your long term happiness and mental health. A word of caution here is that you don't want to overdo it. If you use shopping too much and spend more than you can afford, you will end up with financial issues that can bring about a whole other set of negative consequences.

What else do you like to do for fun? Do you like to take pictures, hike, see new places, or hang out with friends? One suggestion is that you look for an activity that involves other people. It needs to be an activity that will keep your mind engaged and avoid loneliness. Another great idea is trying something new. The perfect activity, and a new passion for you, might be out there waiting for you to discover it.

One way to find other people to hang out with and do things is through online groups. For example, go to www. meetup.com. Once you go to their site, you can search for groups of people who share common interest. There are hiking groups, shopping groups, singles groups, salsa and ballroom dancing groups, foodies groups and many others. The

groups form online, but then get together to talk about or participate in those activities. It is a great way to meet people who share your interest, while enjoying one of your factorize activities.

I'm part of the Triad Photography Meetup group, the Greensboro Tennis Meetup group, and a group called Anything's Possible. In fact, I met my wife Tina through the tennis meetup group. I played weekly with the tennis meetup group for quite a while, and was very involved in the photography group. I even taught classed in Adobe Photoshop at the photography meetup group.

Meetup.com is one way to find new people to hang out with and new things to try, but certainly not the only way. Most towns have community centers where people gather to do different actives and many of these centers provide meeting spaces for groups that meet around specific hobbies or other interest. A simple web search will reveal lots of chances to get out of your house or apartment, meet new people and have a lot of fun.

It is difficult to stay depressed when you are out having fun with other people. You will likely lose track of time, and quite possibly make closer friendships with people you meet in the group(s).

If you don't like crowds, spending time with a large group of people may be the last thing you want to do. There are likely a few friends you do feel comfortable spending time with. Call one of them and do something together. Even if it is sitting at home and reading or watching TV, you aren't doing it alone. If you are into reading, go to a bookstore that has a café like Barnes & Noble and check out a handful of new books. In that environment you are still around others, but aren't forced to interact with a lot of different people. You get some of the benefits of physically getting away from where you are feeling depressed. This simple technique forces you to get off the couch, drive to the book store, talk to a person at the counter and read new material that engages you mentally.

Many book stores have book clubs where you can meet with a very small group of people who enjoy the same types of books you do. It is a much more quiet and intimate environment where you don't feel stressed by a large group of extroverts, but you still get the benefits of being with other people. You can find ways to spend time with others, or do something that engages you mentally and physically without having to feel stressed about meeting and socializing with a lot of people you don't know. It might take a bit more investigation, but you can find an activity that will get you moving and engaged.

Exercise

Another way to get yourself away from negative emotions and depression is to get some exercise. Like going out to have fun, if you are feeling depressed getting physical exercise is the last thing that you want to do. However, it is one of the most beneficial things you can do for yourself physically and emotionally. Studies have shown that physical exercise is as beneficial, and often more beneficial in the longer term, than anti-depressants (Blumenthal, Smith & Hoffman, 2012).

Not only will you get a short term benefit from getting off the couch and exercising right now, exercising regularly will have long-term benefits. You don't have to spend hours in a gym. Five short minutes of aerobic exercise can have big benefits. The ideal is to do at least twenty minutes of aerobic and/or strength exercise three to five times a week. That isn't a big time commitment. Get up a few minutes earlier and go for a walk before work, join a gym and stop on the way home a few days a week, take a yoga class or water aerobics class or join the YMCA and go swimming. All you have to do is get

moving, and your body will release endorphins that will ease depression, lower your blood sugar and blood pressure and help you feel better.

The physical benefits of exercise have been well published, and are touted on nearly every news cast and talk show. Dr. Oz has made millions telling people the benefits of eating better and exercising. I'll touch on these benefits, but they are not the main focus of this book.

What I do want to talk about is time and energy. You can't be exercising and sitting on the couch eating junk food at the same time. Every minute you spend exercising is a minute you aren't eating something you shouldn't or sitting alone obsessing over the abuse you experienced from the bullies. Your mind is not designed to do two things at the same time. It is very difficult to be thinking about your problems while you are focused on exercising.

Not only is it difficult to focus on the trauma from the bullying while exercising, the feel good endorphins your body releases will boost your mood. It will be much easier to focus on the good things in your life and the goals you want to achieve, because your body will be pushing you to have more positive thoughts and emotions.

The strange thing is that when you are sitting on the couch watching television you feel lazy and listless. You feel tired and often get sleepy. When you exercise, however, the opposite happens. As you exercise, your body reacts in a positive way. You may feel tired immediately after exercising, but within a short time you will feel more energetic. It seems counterintuitive, but the more you use energy, the more energy you have. The human body is an amazing machine and the only machine that actually performs better when put under physical stress.

I know many of you are busy. If you are working full time, possibly taking classes while working and have a spouse and/

or kids it can be tough to find time to do the things you enjoy and exercise. But if you don't take care of yourself, you won't be able to take care of those around you as well either.

If you don't feel like you have enough time to exercise and have fun, start keeping a journal. You might be amazed how much time you are wasting in front of the television. One study showed that the average person watches 5 hours of television every day (Hinckley, 2014). You might not spend that much time in front of the TV, but what about tracking how much time you spend on social media and TV combined? Keeping a journal on how you spend your time will help you carve out a time for exercise that will best fit into your schedule.

Making the time to incorporate exercise into your daily routine is easier said than done. Trust me, I struggle to make it a daily habit as much as I should. But you will always find time for what is most important to you. Make time to have fun and incorporate exercise into your life. You will struggle less with depression and the negative emotions from the bullying, which will make you a much happier person to be around. Your friends, spouse and/or children will enjoy being around you more when you are together, and everybody wins.

Chapter 18
Gratitude and Service

The past few rest stops have been based on the concept of dealing with problems that arise as you travel towards your destination. Specifically, these activities were ways to stop going down the road of rumination and negativity.

Along with fixing problems, there is also a need for regular maintenance on your car and your GPS. Keeping them in good condition can prevent major problems farther down the road. If you implement the next few rest stops into your daily life, you will find you struggle much less with negative emotions and thoughts about the bullying and how much the trauma affected your life.

One way to lessen your struggle with memories and pain from the past is to change your focus. Gratitude and service are great ways to change your focus. As you work on making these two rest stops a part of your regular routine, keep in mind that it takes time to change thought patterns developed over years or even decades.

Gratitude

Cultivating more gratitude into your life is worth the small amount of effort involved. It is nearly impossible to be grateful and feel down at the same time. I'm not saying that you can cure depression just by being more grateful, but it can be a break from the depression and possibly keep you from going back there as easily. It is like getting a four wheel alignment on your car. It makes it easier to steer straight when the car isn't pulling to one side.

You may be wondering how you can be grateful when the bullying you suffered in your past has had such negative effects on your life. What can you possibly be grateful for? You may be surprised by the answer to that question. There is a lot you can be thankful for. There is a Persian proverb that states:

> I never lamented about the vicissitudes of time or complained of the turns of fortune except on the occasion when I was barefooted and unable to procure slippers. But when I entered the great mosque of Kufah with a sore heart and beheld a man without feet I offered thanks to the bounty of God, consoled myself for my want of shoes…

Most people have heard this proverb in various forms, but it might cause you to stop and think about all that you have to be grateful for. Do your arms and legs work? Is your eyesight normal, your hearing normal and other senses working? Do you have a roof over your head and food to eat? Do you have a car to get where you need to go? Do you have more clothes than you need and more than one pair of shoes? If you answered yes to these questions, you are better off than most people in the world.

Every day that you are alive, you have a lot to be grateful for. If you really want to see how good you have it, spend a short amount of time in a nursing home. A lot of the people there appear physically helpless. Many of them can't get out of bed without help and struggle with multiple physical ailments. Yet, a surprising number of them are still upbeat.

So, what else do you have to be grateful for? Do you have friends and/or family members who love and care for you? If you have family and friends who love you, you are indeed very blessed.

Are you in a relationship or married? Are there hobbies or sports that you enjoy and people who you enjoy doing these things with? Do you have a computer and access to the internet? The fact that you can read this book puts you ahead of many people living in less developed parts of the world.

I challenge you to start with a list of these very basic things, write them down and refer to them every day. You can either do this in the morning or evening, but creating this list in the morning is a great way to start your day off on a positive note. It can also be useful to look at this list several times a day. When you sense negative thoughts and memories encroaching on your thinking, you can refer back to it.

Now, begin to add to the list things that either will happen or have happened the day before. It's often the little things that are the most meaningful. For example, did you get a compliment from your boss on a project you were working on, or did someone you look up to have a positive word to say to you? Did your commute to work go better and quicker than usual, or did your spouse or significant other do something that showed how much he/she cared? Did your child or children do something that made you smile? Tings that most people don't pay attention to can be reasons to be thankful (for example, getting a great parking spot at a store or getting through the checkout line quickly at the grocery store).

I recently got a chance to attend am event with Tina that made me very grateful. Neither of us had gone to our high school proms. A radio station in our community had a prom to raise money for breast cancer research. It was a retro prom with an 80's theme. Since we both graduated in the 80's, we decided to go. I dressed like Don Johnson in Miami Vice, and Tina dressed like Molly Ringwald from Pretty in Pink. We had a lot of fun, and it felt like a piece of our youth that had been taken away from both of us was restored. We were just dancing and enjoying ourselves, but there was a sense that something wrong in our past had been made right. This will be a memory that I will choose to dwell on often when I find myself feeling like I was robbed of good memories from my youth.

Being more grateful is a matter of changing your focus. Instead of spending your time and mental energy focusing on what you don't have, you choose to be grateful for what you do have.

As you take the time to keep a daily journal of what you have to be thankful for, you will develop a new habitual way of thinking. Your journal will become much like a maintenance log for your vehicle. This preventative maintenance will not only keep your car running smoother for your trip, it will aid in further reprogramming your mind or GPS. Instead of looking for things in your life that are wrong or looking at events through a negative or victim mindset, you will look at the experiences in your life through a much less distorted lens. You will be seeking opportunities to see the positives in your daily life.

Eventually, you might not need to write down the things you are grateful for. It will become your mentality and you will have committed most of the things you are grateful for to memory. You will be able to go to your list of all the things you are grateful for anytime you need the boost.

This positive and grateful outlook will keep you from being pulled off course by the negative events that you will experience in your life. Even when you experience something as tragic as the death of a loved one, you will be able to get back on the right road much more quickly. You will be able to look back and see the bigger picture. Instead of getting stuck in the grieving process, after a reasonable time you will be able to focus on the future.

Service

Along with changing your attitude, stepping out and taking actions that reinforce the more positive mindset can be a wonderful way to keep your car on the right road. One of the best actions you can take is to engage physically and mentally in something that is bigger than yourself.

Serving others not only connects you with a cause bigger than yourself, it will likely make you a happier person overall. To get the biggest benefit, your service needs to not have any payback. It needs to be as selfless as possible. When you serve others, you take your focus from the internal to the external. Service often means helping people who have less money than you, physical disabilities or other problems that are much more severe than your own.

Serving others, especially those who have less than you do, has tremendous benefits. You will feel needed and appreciated. There will be a sense of accomplishing something that improves the lives of others and feel good about yourself as a person. You may make contacts and/or friendships with other volunteers and the people you are helping, which adds to your social connections. One lasting benefit is that serving others can boost your long-term happiness (Phillips, 2014).

Serving others even has some surprising health benefits. According to the Huffington Post, volunteering can lead to a longer life, help with pain management and lower blood pressure (Goldman, 2014).

There are many different ways to serve others. These can include working directly with people such as serving food at a soup kitchen or handing out blankets and other supplies to the homeless. There is always a place for those who like to work directly with those in need. You may, however, be more comfortable working with things than people. There is a need for your abilities as well. For example, my father, Glyn, volunteers every Friday morning at the Second Harvest Food Bank. He spends about 3 hours sorting through cartons of eggs donated by local grocery stores. Glyn goes through these cartons of eggs, and sorts the good eggs from the broken ones. This food bank feeds more than 300,000 families in this area every year, and fresh eggs are a wonderful source of high quality protein for them. He doesn't work directly with the people he helps in this position, but what he does is critical to the food bank.

If you are good with numbers, you can help with office work at a non-profit. Maybe you could sort donated clothes and other items at a local Goodwill store or Salvation Army store. You could build houses for Habitat for Humanity. There are thousands of ways you can help. One phone call to a local United Way or going to http://www.volunteermatch. org and doing a quick search will reveal more opportunities than you could have imagined. I can guarantee there is an organization that has a need that matches your skills and abilities.

Every suggestion in this book is like a two sided coin. Even with good things, there is the potential for some negatives. What negatives could there possibly be to doing good things for others? I'm glad you asked.

As a person who experienced bullying, you were subjected to rejection and social isolation. It is natural for you to want everyone to like you. Once you start volunteering, you will receive a lot of positive encouragement and accolades

from people within the organizations where you are lending a hand. They won't have any malice about it, but they will likely ask you to help on projects beyond the time commitment you made with them. You won't want to say no, because part of you will be enjoying the praise and friendship.

If you start saying yes to too many projects, you can find yourself in danger of burning out. You can take on too many projects in an attempt to be everything to everyone. This can lead to not finishing all the projects you have taken on, and that can make you feel like a failure.

You will need to understand your own time limits, needs and abilities. Remember a few pages ago when I was talking about having fun and physical exercise, I told you that if you don't take care of yourself you won't have the energy to be able to take care of the other people and commitments in your life? The same is true here. You want to help other people, but you need time to do things that recharge your batteries. You will be more effective if you aren't exhausted from being overcommitted.

You are going to have to learn to use a word that might be a little difficult to say at first: NO. One strategy is to not give an answer on the spot. If someone asks you to help, put a note in your smartphone or ask them to email the request to you. That will give you a chance to talk with your spouse or other people in your life about the other things you have committed yourself to. Together you can evaluate if this is something that you have adequate time for and if it fits in with your other life goals. If you don't have the time to take on another project, it will be easier to say no.

You may still struggle with feeling like people won't like you if you say no. However, in my case, I have found the opposite to be true. Because I only take on commitments I am truly passionate about and limit my number of commitments, I am able to give my full attention to those projects. The result is better quality work, If anyone rejects me because I can't help, they weren't truly my friends in the first place.

Try to maintain a healthy balance. Helping others will provide far more rewards to you than to those you help. But remember to give yourself time to do what you love and not get burned out being there for everyone. If you are married, ask your spouse to help you manage your commitments. If you are single, ask a close friend to help you know when to say no.

Chapter 19
Religious Affiliation

When you read the title to this chapter, it might have triggered some negative associations. Maybe you were raised in a particular religion, a new age philosophy or possibly an agnostic or atheistic home. It is possible that you have had negative experiences related to one organized religion or religious group. If so, these negative experiences may have turned you away from the idea of God, the Universe or any ideas that have to do with seeking to be part of a cause bigger than yourself.

If the last paragraph describes you, I'm going to ask you to drop any pre-conceived notions of spirituality and approach this idea with an open mind. I'm not going to preach one particular religious belief at you. You read in my story that I am a person of faith, and that my faith has helped me through some of the issues I struggled with, and still struggle with, from the bullying. However, I will attempt to approach this with as little bias as possible.

As you continue to move from where you were to where you ultimately want to go, you may find that you need help when your car breaks down. This is when religious affiliation can aid you in getting back on the road, and further defining where you want to go.

Seeking to be part of something bigger than yourself, and/or being more spiritual can have many benefits. In fact,

Most studies have shown that religious involvement and spirituality are associated with better health outcomes, including greater longevity, coping skills, and health-related quality of life (even during terminal illness) and less anxiety, depression, and suicide (Mueller, 2001).

The benefits this author mentioned are closely associated with active involved in a church, mosque, temple or other religious affiliation. Similar to serving others, spending time with people in a religious setting helps you focus beyond yourself. Most religious organizations spend time seeking guidance from a higher power, and devote themselves to serving others. These types of activities refocus your attention away from your own internal struggles.

As you take part in activities that emphasize being part of something bigger than yourself and helping others, you might discover new directions that you hadn't considered before. There may be a career path or relationship that you had been unaware of. You will also see the road ahead from a broader perspective, which helps you make better decisions about the next stage of your journey.

Another benefit of getting involved in a religious organization is being around other people who share similar core values. One of the worst things you can do when you are struggling with depression or painful memories from the bullying is to sit alone with your thoughts. Being in a large church or mosque where you are in a crowd of strangers is not ideal, but it is still better than being alone. However, you won't get the full benefit of religious affiliation with this type of involvement.

Smaller groups are where you are more likely to develop lasting and more positive relationships. These small groups will likely have a focus much larger than your own problems. Being part of a small group will provide you opportunities to serve together. You will get the feel good benefits of helping others, plus a sense of belonging to the group.

Small groups are where you develop friendships with people who support each other in difficult times and celebrate together when one or more members of the group achieve goals or reach milestones. Most of these groups keep the information shared among members confidential, making the group a safe place for members to share things they are struggling with and receive support. The sense of belonging and support can have benefits that last far beyond the short time you spend meeting as a group. Individual members or couples within these groups often spend time together socially outside of the group setting. This reinforces the friendships and sense of community.

The benefits of involvement with a religious organization, and particularly involvement in a small group, far outweigh the negatives. Yes, you will occasionally run into people within any organized religion that have a holier than thou type of attitude, and there are hypocrites in every religious organization. There are even a few people who use religious groups to get close to people and take advantage of them. Most of these people don't stay in one group very long because their motives become clear and they leave. Despite these negatives, involvement with a religious group can help you recover more quickly from traumatic life events and generally improve your emotional and physical health.

If you find a larger religious organization that you are drawn to, visit several of the small groups. See if there is one where you not only feel welcomed, but where you seem to gel with individuals from the group. It may take time to

find a group where you can make strong connections, but the connections you make there may help tremendously as you continue to discover and travel towards your ultimate destination.

Chapter 20
Meditation/Prayer

Religious affiliation is a group or corporate activity that provides external benefits, meditation and/or prayer, however, is more solitary. It can help you change your thoughts and attitudes helping you stay focused on the road ahead.

The mind generates a nearly constant stream of thoughts. Some are chosen on a conscious level, but many seem to be generated by the sub-conscious. These thoughts have a tendency to jump around at random like popcorn popping. No wonder it is easy to go off course. You hear your internal voice and see images flash through your mind so fast that it is hard to keep up.

Most religions emphasize some type of prayer or meditation. Taking the time to focus on one thought, one diety or your breathing takes discipline. However, the benefits are well worth it. Meditation increases immune function, decreases pain, boost your happiness level, reduces stress and increases your ability to control your emotions.

One of the goals of meditation or prayer is to quiet the mind. You see this in multiple religions. For example, in the Jewish and Christian faith, the Bible tells readers to "Be still, and know that I am God" (Psalm 46:10).

The discipline learned through the practice of medication or prayer goes far beyond the practice itself. As Buddha stated, "There is nothing so disobedient as an undisciplined mind, and there is nothing so obedient as a disciplined mind." As you meditate or pray you will begin to take mastery over your thoughts. This will make it easier to avoid the negative thoughts, even when you aren't meditating. The discipline will also help you in your job and personal life.

A quick search online will reveal lots of suggestions on prayer or meditation. Here are a few from well-respected practitioners:

http://www.chopra.com/ccl-meditation/21dmc/meditation-tips.html

http://www.dalailama.com/teachings/training-the-mind/verse-8

https://www.joycemeyer.org/articles/ea.aspx?article=the_truth_about_prayer

http://billygraham.org/answer/does-god-only-hear-us-when-we-pray-out-loud-or-does-he-hear-silent-prayers-also/

Not only does meditation or prayer help you get control of your thoughts, it connects you with a higher power. Regargless of whether you subscribe to an organized religion or believe in the power of the universe, prayer and meditation will help you feel more connected. This can not only help you avoid negative thoughts, it can lessen loneliness and depression.

Many people who teach meditation focus on breathing as a part of the process. It may seem a little silly. After all, breathing is something you do without thinking about it. But do you really breathe in a way that has the most benefit to your body? Breathing techniques from meditation bring more oxygen into your body, slow your heart rate and lower your blood pressure. Plus, taking the time to focus on your breathing calms your mind's chatter. As you focus on your breathing, the stresses of work, family life and the trauma from the bullying will bother you less.

So when you are struggling to focus on where you want to be, take time to meditate or pray. Focus on your breathing and try to connect with a higher power. You will find that those few minutes will likely leave you feeling more refreshed and ready to get back on the road.

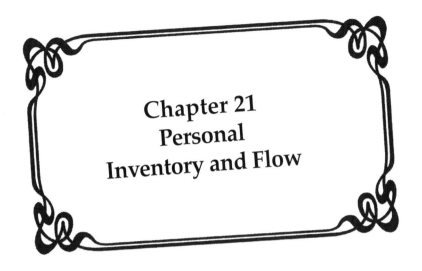

Chapter 21
Personal
Inventory and Flow

The gratitude rest stop encouraged you to take an inventory of the good things in your life. The major focus of this inventory, aside from physical health, was the external things you have to be grateful for. The positive personal inventory, however, has a much more internal focus.

You might still find it easy to look back at your life and see the failures rather than the triumphs. The bullies spent a great deal of time and effort convincing you that you are worthless and pointing out your faults. Most of the negative coping mechanisms were directly related to the low self-esteem that the bullies tried to instill in you.

If you take a more objective look at yourself, you will likely find that there are a lot of positive things about you and good things that you have accomplished. A great place to start is to look at your natural talents. Are you creative, intelligent, or have good analytical skills? Do you have physical skills that make you good at sports or able to do certain jobs better than others?

Are you naturally organized? If so, I'm jealous.

What about your interpersonal skills. Are you naturally

outgoing or kind? Do you empathize easily with others? Are you able to help people in need and bring comfort? Are you reliable and dependable? Are you punctual?

Next, look at not who you are but what you've done. Take some time to think about people you have helped or ways that you have made the world a better place. Have you given time or money to charity? Have you been there for someone who needed a friend, or helped family members who were in need? Have you been a good employee at one or more jobs, or managed to finish a college degree? Have you accomplished a lot in your career, or managed to earn a great living for you and/or your family?

As you write these things down, make a conscious decision to like the person you are. Yes, you have made mistakes, but you have also done good things in your time on earth. You are a unique individual with unique talents and abilities that can be used to improve the lives of others.

It is very difficult to love and hate at the same time. Give yourself permission to love who you are as well as who you can be. As you begin to look for things to like about yourself, you will be better able to see the opportunities in front of you. You will be able to focus on the road ahead instead of the negative words in your self-talk. This will boost your confidence making you better equipped to risk trying new things and traveling down unfamiliar roads.

Flowing

The last rest stop is flow. Imagine you are at the start of a 100 meter dash. As you crouch down, you place your feet on the starting blocks and feel your fingers touching the ground. All sounds seem to disappear except your breathing and heartbeat. The starting pistol fires. As you push off the starting block and build speed, you can feel the wind rushing by your ears. The sense of time falls away and you get tunnel vision as you push forward with every muscle in your body. As you break the tape at the finish line, you nearly collapse and the sense of timelessness goes away. You become aware of the other runners, the crowd cheering and your own exhaustion. For the few seconds you were running, you were totally lost in the moment.

The scenario just described is an example of what some counselors call flow. Many people refer to this as being in the zone. It is often experienced in sports such as tennis, soccer and basketball. Writers have been known to become inspired and spend hours writing without taking a break to eat. Many artist and musicians experience flow when they are expressing themselves through their crafts. It can almost bring a sense of euphoria.

Everyone experiences flow in some activity. For example, when I'm working in Photoshop I hyper focus and often lose track of time. I will look up and realize that I've spent hours working on a project.

You are most likely to experience flow when the activity:
- Is challenging enough to require your full attention but not so challenging that it is overwhelming
- Has clear goals and/or rules
- Provides immediate feedback
- Uses your natural talents and abilities

One of the best indications that you are or have experienced flow is that you become so engrossed that you lose track of time. Think back to an activity you enjoy doing and has enough challenge to it that any sense of time disappears. Flow often brings better than average performance because you are singularly focused on the activity.

Flow and overall happiness appear to be linked, but what isn't as concrete is the cause and effect relationship. It's the chicken and egg question. Do we experience more flow be-

cause we are happy, or are we happier because we have more flow experiences?

Flow is another way to deal with the road block of depression. When you find you are stuck and struggling with depression, go do something that has brought you a sense of flow in the past. Flow experiences can take you completely out of your internal dialogue. When you are experiencing flow, you are so focused on what you are doing you tune out nearly everything but the activity you are engaged in. Similar to using the power of choice and exercise, flow experiences get you out of your own head and your mind off of your problems.

Engaging in activities that bring a sense of flow on a regular basis has one other big benefit. To experience flow, you must be involved in an activity that truly challenges you. When you push yourself and take on new challenges, especially challenges that use your natural abilities, you will often experience success and have a sense of accomplishment. You will then need to push yourself to the next level and reach another plateau. Every success takes you further down the road to a happier and more successful you.

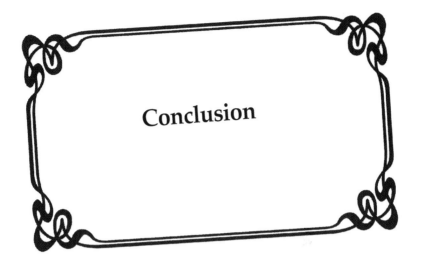

Conclusion

Your ultimate road trip is just getting started. You have miles of road with amazing scenery ahead of you. You will meet a lot of interesting people who will help you along the way and point out new destinations that you might want to visit. You've hopefully started the healing process, so the painful memories and issues form the bullying are becoming nothing more than a part of your past that you see in your rear view mirror.

If you are still struggling with some of the issues from the past, it's ok. Please be patient with yourself as you go through this process. Change doesn't happen overnight. You might have been bullied for years and spent more time ruminating over the trauma you experienced at the hands of the bullies. You've also had years, and possibly decades, of practice perfecting a negative thought process. Everything and everyone in your life might be viewed through the prism of pain and trauma. Up to this point in your life this prism has distorted how you see the world and the people around you.

My story illustrates that healing and achieving dreams is possible, but it took time. It was over ten years from the time that I realized I needed healing till I felt I had truly made it past the trauma from the bullying.

It will be helpful to find a friend or counselor to as you continue the healing process, That person can be there to support yo u and help you identify where you want to go and how best to get there. You might have to deal with some pretty rough roads and run into roadblocks as you deal with the trauma from the bullying. A friend or counselor can also help you keep moving forward rather than getting stuck in the past.

As you identify where you want to be and plan your route, you will be amazed at what great destinations you find along the way and how much fun you will have on the journey. Don't worry about detours. Sometimes detours take you to wonderful places that you would never have known about without them.

Congratulations on your commitment to healing form the past and taking the initiative to start on your new road trip. You can and will overcome the pain from the bullying, and you are likely to go farther than you ever imagined.

Resources

http://www.stopbullying.gov/get-help-now/ - Government anti-bullying website

http://www.pacerkidsagainstbullying.org/kab/ - Kids Against Bullying – Non-profit organization dedicated to ending bullying in schools

http://www.stompoutbullying.org/ - Stomp Out Bullying – The Leading National Bullying and Cyberbullying Prevention Organization for Kids & Teens

http://www.nami.org/ - NAMI (National Alliance on Mental Illness)

http://www.freedomfromfear.org/FindingTreatment.en.html - Freedom from Fear – organization that helps those struggling with depression find help and healing.

http://www.nimh.nih.gov/index.shtml - National Institute of Mental Health

http://nobullying.com/category/bullying-facts/anti-bullying/?submit=Go – List of resources to help victims of bullying from NoBullying.com

Bibliography

Achor, S. (2010). The happiness advantage: the seven principles of positive psychology that fuel success and performance at work. New York: Broadway Books.

Adams, S. (2014, June 20). Most Americans Are Unhappy At Work. Retrieved September 10, 2015, from http://www.forbes.com/sites/susanadams/2014/06/20/most-americans-are-un-happy-at-work/

Atalay, S. (2008, October 15). Small splurges, large benefits. Retrieved November 14, 2015, from http://www.hec.edu/Knowledge/Marketing/Consumer-Behavior/Small-splurg-es-large-benefits

Blanco, J. (2013). It's NOT Just Joking Around! - A Survivor's Guide to Joking and Peer Abuse :: Jodee Blanco. Retrieved September 29, 2015, from http://www.jodeeblanco.com/sur-vival_adults.htm

Blumenthal, J. A., Smith, P. J., & Hoffman, B. M. (2012). Is Exercise a Viable Treatment for Depression? ACSM's Health & Fitness Journal, 16(4), 14–21. Retrieved April 5, 2015 from http://doi.org/10.1249/01.FIT.0000416000.09526.eb

Bowen, W. (2007). A complaint free world: how to stop complaining and start enjoying the life you always wanted. New York: Doubleday.

Bullying Statistics. (2015). Retrieved September 20, 2015, from http://www.bullyingstatistics.org/content/bullying-and-sui-cide.html

Carlisle, N., & Rofes, E. (2007). School bullying: Do adult survivors perceive long-term effects? Traumatology, 13(1), 16-26. Retrieved from http://tmt.sagepub.com/content/13/1/16

Douglas Vanderbilt, Marilyn Augustyn, The effects of bullying, Pediatrics and Child Health, volume 20, issue 7, July 2010, Pages 315–320, http://dx.doi.org/10.1016/j.paed.2010.03.008

Freedhoff, Y. (2013, January 30). Does It Only Take 3 Weeks to

Form a Habit? Rethinking the popular claim that habits form in 21 days. US News. Retrieved July 28, 2014, from http://health.usnews.com/health-news/blogs/eat-run/2013/01/30/does-it-only-take-3-weeks-to-form-a-habit

Gillett, R. (2015, October 7). How Walt Disney, Oprah Winfrey, and 19 Other Successful People Rebounded After Getting Fired. Retrieved November 13, 2015, from http://www.inc.com/business-insider/21-successful-people-who-rebounded-after-getting-fired.html

Goldman, L. (2014, January 14). 4 Amazing Health Benefits Of Helping Others. Retrieved September 17, 2015, from http://www.huffingtonpost.com/2013/12/28/health-benefits-of-helping-others_n_4427697.html

Heid, M. (2014, April 30). Your Brain On: Bullying. Retrieved July 29, 2014, from http://www.shape.com/lifestyle/mind-and-body/your-brain-bullying

Hewlett, S., & Luce, C. (2006). Extreme Jobs: The Dangerous Allure of the 70-Hour Workweek. Harvard Business Review. Retrieved January 17, 2015 from https://hbr.org/2006/12/extreme-jobs-the-dangerous-allure-of-the-70-hour-workweek

Hinckley, D. (2014, March 5). Average American watches 5 hours of TV per day. New York Daily News Retrieved September 23, 2015, from http://www.nydailynews.com/life-style/average-american-watches-5-hours-tv-day-article-1.1711954

Hyman, M.D., M. (2004, February 14). White poison: The danger of sugar - and how to beat it. New York Daily News. Retrieved September 21, 2015, from http://www.nydailynews.com/life-style/health/white-poison-danger-sugar-beat-article-1.1605232

Jantzer, A. M., Hoover, J. H., & Narloch, R. (2006, May). Quality of friendships in young adulthood: A preliminary research note the relationship between school-aged bullying and trust, shyness and quality of friendships in young adulthood: A preliminary research note. School Psychology International, 27(2), 146-156.

Lyubomirsky, S. (2008). The how of happiness: a scientific approach to getting the life you want. New York: Penguin Press.

Mueller, P. S., Plevak, D. J., & Rummans, T. A. (2001). Religious involvement, spirituality, and medicine: Implications for clinical practice. Mayo Clinic Proceedings, 76(12), 1225-35. Retrieved from http://search.proquest.com/docview/216882150?accountid=458

Outlaw, Frank. (1977 May 18), San Antonio Light, What They're Saying, Quote Page 7-B (NArch Page 28), Column 4, San Antonio, Texas. (Newspaper Archive)

Pappas, S. (2013, February 20). The Pain of Bullying Lasts into Adulthood. Retrieved September 20, 2015, from http://www.livescience.com/27279-bullying-effects-last-adulthood.html

Phillips, Edward M.D. Simple Changes, Big Rewards: A practical, easy guide for healthy, happy living - Harvard Health. (2014).

Smith, Peter K;Singer, Monika;Hoel, Helge;Cooper, Cary L. Victimization in the school and the workplace: Are there any links? British Journal of Psychology; May 2003; 94.
Smith, S. (2010, October 11). Avoid The Trap Overachieving, Feeling Underappreciated Can Lead To Burnout. Tribune Business News. Retrieved March 8, 2014, from http://search.proquest.com/docview/757192685?accountid=458

Sourander A, Jensen P, Ronning JA, et al. What is the early adulthood outcome of boys who bully or are bullied in childhood? The Finnish "From a Boy to a Man" study. Pediatrics 2007, 120 (2), 397–404.

Student Reports of Bullying and Cyber-Bullying: Results From the 2011 School Crime Supplement to the National Crime Victimization Survey. (2013, September 1). Retrieved November

9, 2015, from http://nces.ed.gov/pubs2013/2013329.pdf

Vanderbilt, Douglas, Marilyn, Augustyn, The effects of bullying, Pediatrics and Child Health, Volume 20, Issue 7, July 2010, Pages 315–320, http://dx.doi.org/10.1016/j.paed.2010.03.008

Vámosi, M. (2012). Being bullied during childhood and the risk of obesity in adulthood: A co-twin control study. Health, 4(12A), 1537-1545.

Weiner-Bronner, D. (2010, September 29). Rutgers Student Believed To Have Committed Suicide After Classmates Allegedly Recorded Him In Gay Sexual Encounter. Huffington Post. Retrieved from http://www.huffingtonpost.com/2010/09/29/dharun-revi-molly-wei-charged_n_743539.html

Wilson, L. (2013, September 26). Louisiana Teen Deaths Highlight Dangers of Bullying. USA Today. Retrieved from http://www.usatoday.com/story/news/nation/2013/09/25/student-bullying-suicides/2867781/

About the Author

Mark Stewart has over twenty years of experience as a professional photographer, designer and writer. He has a Bachelor's degree in English and a Master's degree in Mass Communications and Media Arts from Southern Illinois University in Carbondale, Illinois.

In the last ten years, Mark has shifted his focus from marketing to teaching and helping others. He has taught classes for Winston-Salem State University, AIU online and the University of Phoenix. He has also taught workshops to help people overcome adversity and create lives that have deep personal meaning and success.

He lives in Winston-Salem, North Carolina with his wife Tina and son Joel. He enjoys playing tennis, photography, bowling and traveling with Tina.

You can contact mark through his website at mark@dauntless-press.com or through Facebook at https://www.facebook.com/nameswillneverhurt/

Made in the USA
Charleston, SC
31 March 2016